GIVE.
LIVE.
SAVE.

The First Three Disciplines Needed to Win
in Your Finances

RANDY BOWEN

Copyright © 2022 Randy Bowen
All rights reserved
First Edition

Fulton Books
Meadville, PA

Published by Fulton Books 2022

ISBN 978-1-63860-950-6 (paperback)
ISBN 978-1-63860-951-3 (digital)

Printed in the United States of America

First and foremost, I want to thank you for picking up this book! Although this book can be read by anyone, and will create value to all who pick it up, *Give. Live. Save.* will bring the most value for people who have just started to look into their finances or those who are looking for a unique take on the subject. If you are a person living paycheck to paycheck or just above and just struggle to gain ground in their finances, this book is for you! I am here to give you real honest, counterintuitive financial concepts that will help you build discipline and ultimately win in your finances.

You will notice in the book that in a lot of sections, I use direct language like "you" and "your" instead of more collective language like "us" and "we." The reason for this is because I wrote this book for you, the reader, directly, and I want it to feel more like a one-on-one conversation rather than a mass address. The word "you" sometimes can come across as harsh or judgmental, but that is not the intent. I want you to hear that although you may have made some of these financial mistakes, you are still truly your biggest asset to winning in your finances, and my only intent is to give you some extra tools to get you to the finish line!

Winning in your finances is not a get-rich-quick scheme. It takes countercultural thinking, hard work, and the ability to adjust and take things one step at a time. What does winning in your finances look like? It looks like thinking differently, building disciplines, and winning the war on debt. Trust me, it is a whole new world after you get out of debt, and you will get there! But let's start with the three big disciplines that need to be built to win this financial game. The first one is give. Giving is all about leading your life with open hands, changing your perspective, and learning how to live on less than you make. Live. Live is all about prioritizing your life, making sure your family is taken care of and stays your top priority. Within the category of live, you will learn how to win the war on debt and get yourself on solid ground. Save. Planning for the future but also taking advantage of the present by using your own money to cover emergencies and pay for your life! This is winning! Every good small discipline you create in your financial situation is a win. Put enough of these small disciplines together, you won't only win the war on debt, but you will win in your finances and create disciplines that will transform your life.

My hope is after you have implemented these disciplines in your personal finances, you will intentionally find new ways to implement them into your daily life!

Money Touches Everything

When I was thinking about turning these concepts into a book, I had to figure out why someone would benefit from these concepts in more areas than just finance. I've noticed a couple trends when I talk to people about their financial situations. People who open up about their financial situations are more willing to share about other areas of their life. Although money touches everything, money is more often the symptom, and once you deal with it, it can reveal the root cause of your pain. My hope for this book is that you will not only win financially, but it will cause you to win in other areas of your life as well. We will mainly cover the financial side of these disciplines, but as you build and grow in these disciplines, you will find that they will influence the rest of your life as well!

It's important to understand that money touches everything in our lives. There are very few, if any, areas that money does not play a role in. From the clothes we wear, the cars we drive, the vacations we take, and the lives we lead, money is present. Existing without money in this society is impossible. We can't go anywhere or do anything without it. Sure, we could walk somewhere, but we need clothes and shoes to do that. Zig Ziglar was quoted saying, "Money is not the most important thing in life, but it ranks pretty high up with oxygen on the 'got to have it' scale."

Gone are the days where we could trade product for product to survive. We now trade money for products or services. Our marriage takes money, our relationships take money, everything takes money. This isn't a bad thing. We just have to understand that if money touches everything in our lives, then making money work for us is incredibly important to win in all areas of life. When talking to married couples, finances are often the first causes of stress in their marriages. So much so that when surveyed, 68 percent of married couples said that money fights were their number one reason for wanting a divorce; that is just above infidelity.[1] "According to a new national study conducted on behalf of the FP Canada, women are significantly more likely than men to lose sleep over financial worries while the study found that 42% of Canadians (excluding Quebecers) rank money as their greatest stress."[2]

These stats are not meant to scare, just simply to show how important it is to get this money thing right. With so much tension around the subject of money, we need to understand how important it is to learn to control it and not let it control us. Money is a necessity for us to survive, but we need to use it as a tool, and not something that has control over us instead.

Before we dive into the individual concepts, we have to understand that dealing with finances, it is less about money and more about our behavior with it. It's a discipline problem before it becomes a math problem. There is a reason why 70 percent of people who win the lottery end up bankrupt in a few years.[3]

More money will not guarantee financial success; creating the proper discipline can. When you look at your financial situation, you need to see it as a need to create financial discipline first before seeing it as a math and/or income problem. I am not here to promise that simply building financial disciplines at your income level will solve

---

[1] Goldhart, C., *Top 5 Reasons for Divorce in Canada | Toronto Family Law | Goldhart & Associates.* Toronto Family Law | Goldhart & Associates. 2015. Available at http://goldhartlaw.com/top-5-reasons-for-divorce-in-canada/. Accessed September 5, 2021.

[2] Financial Planning for Canadians. *Why Women Stress More About Money (Video)—Financial Planning for Canadians.* 2021. Available at https://www.financialplanningforcanadians.ca/financial-planning/why-women-stress-more-about-money?rq=42%25. Accessed September 5, 2021.

[3] Loewenstein, G. *Five Myths About the Lottery. The Washington Post.* 2019. Available at https://www.washingtonpost.com/outlook/five-myths/five-myths-about-the-lottery/2019/12/27/742b9662-2664-11ea-ad73-2fd294520e97_story.html). Accessed September 5, 2021.

all your problems; you may need to do both. "Money is 80% behavior change and 20% a math problem."[4]

Regardless if a higher income is needed or not, I want to make it clear that I am not just talking about income. The income is the most obvious place to start, but it expands into almost every other area of finances as well. When I talk about numbers and guidelines within these concepts of give, live, save, the numbers noted are there for a reason, and the closer someone can get to those numbers, the bigger impact they can make on their financial goals. These numbers should not be looked down on as legalistic. The last thing I want to happen is for someone to give up because they couldn't make the math work. For example, I talk about and recommend giving 10 percent first. There is a good reason why I used 10 percent, and you should make an effort to get as close to that percentage as possible. This may be difficult to do, especially the first few tries. So although 10 percent will give the most benefits, maybe it will have to take a couple months to get there, or maybe the percentage of giving will have to drop it to 5 percent until some breathing room is gained before boosting it up! It is less about the percentage and more about understanding the concepts and making sure giving is alloted its proper place on the priority list.

---

[4] Ramsey, D. https://patch.com/new-hampshire/concord-nh/personal-finance-is-80-behavior-and-only-20-head-knowledge-dave-ramsey.

Finances Are Personal, It's in the Name

Everyone's situation is different and therefore may need a unique approach to get them winning. For instance, one of our clients wanted to buy a home. Through looking over her budget and running the numbers, there was no way she could get to our recommended guidelines for a mortgage (under 25 percent of your take-home pay and paid off in under fifteen years). She lived in a very expensive city, and therefore the housing market is quite inflated. We figured out that for a starter home, she would be looking at around 30 percent of her income if she wanted it paid off in fifteen years. After some more thought, we figured out that with her current income situation, it would make sense to get a small mortgage and pay it off in twenty years instead of fifteen. This would allow her to keep her expenses lower and be able to put her kid through school in the process. Cookie-cutter approaches don't always work, but they are still a good guide to keep you on the proper track to succeed.

In the budget I have created to help you navigate your finances, I have housing listed at 30 percent. This may look like a low percentage, but the bigger concept here is that you keep your big expense as low as you can to help you win in all areas of your finances. This will encourage you not to overspend. This is a guideline where the closer you can get to that number, the better off you will be. When you view this as a blanket statement, you may get stuck thinking it is a math problem to give up before even getting started. When you can see the bigger picture, you can see it as a strong and beneficial guideline to strive for. Do not get discouraged if you can't make the math work; there may be other areas in your finances that you can cut to have things balance out!

Less Math, More Discipline

I AM NOT ASKING FOR perfection. You just started this journey, but I am just asking for you to give this a try. Give 10 percent away right at the beginning, put food on the table, and save some money. (Give. Live. Save.) Then go down the rest of your budget. If you have to come back and adjust, adjust. If you have to sell something or work some overtime, it will be well worth it! If you can't get there this month, do what you can, and make it a goal to hit next month!

It doesn't matter what income you have—anyone can struggle with financial discipline. I have talked with a lot of different people in a lot of different situations and income levels. People with higher incomes and people with lower incomes. There is a different struggle for both, and both need to create the disciplines first! No matter what income level you are, I bet you have said these words at some point and time: if only I made more money. More money is a great asset when you can handle more of what you currently have. Unfortunately, what often happens is your lifestyle rises, and you just continue to add more payments. If you are undisciplined with a small paycheck, you are going to be undisciplined with a bigger one. More money makes you more of what you already are. If finances were strictly a math problem, we wouldn't have broke millionaires. If finances were strictly a math problem, we would think logically and wouldn't carry credit cards. The good as well as the bad news is it's not all math: fix the discipline then make the math work!

Get Clear on Your Motivation, Get Clear on Your Why

Before we even start to talk about the three big disciplines you should create, we need to become laser-focused on our motivation for wanting to win financially. Another way of saying this is we need to know the why behind why we want to win. When we understand why in any situation, we are more willing and able to endure what we have to do to make that why happen. Our why will also help us determine what we need to do to get started. When it comes to building financial discipline, we need to have a big why. The bigger why we have, the more intense we will become to create and stick with the discipline to win in any area of our finances. The larger your why, and the more crystal clear you make your why, the less likely you are to quit early, and not complete your goals![5] Here are a few good questions to ask yourself when trying to get yourself motivated and figure out your why. What scares you about your current financial state? What keeps you up at night, financially or otherwise? Then ask yourself, what are my goals and ambitions in life? What gets you up in the morning?

Maybe you're scared about not making it to the end of the month, not being able to afford your next emergency, or maybe you're scared you'll always live paycheck to paycheck and will never be able to retire. Whatever keeps you up at night, write it down. Then ask yourself, if there was nothing holding me back, not even

---

[5] Sinek, S. *Start with Why* (New York: Portfolio/Penguin, 2009), pp. 65–70.

money, what would I be doing? What would I want my future to look like? This will give you a basic starting point to set some goals for you and your family and, better yet, to give you the motivation to reach those goals, your why!

Based on the examples above, maybe your why is you wanting to change your family tree and be the first one in your family to retire early. Maybe your why is so you don't leave your kids with your debt. Maybe your why is because you never want to ask for money from anyone ever again. Whatever your why is, make it bigger, make it clearer, and make it create some urgency in your life.

It's so easy to find yourself undisciplined in your finances, but it is impossible to gain the proper discipline you need to win without the right motivation, without a big-enough why. This isn't a new concept; lots of authors talk about this in some way, shape, or form. Simon Sinek is one of the authors that teaches this very clearly. Figure out your why, your motivation, then move on to how you are going to make that why happen.

Leading with your why is such a counterintuitive idea, especially when you are dealing with your finances. Most people only deal with the what, the money side of finance. They say things like "I need a better income," "If only I won the lottery," or the worst one yet, "The government will look after me!" Once people realize they aren't getting a raise anytime soon, the lottery is costing them money, and the government doesn't want to help, they will start to finally think about dealing with how they make their financial goals happen. How can I get myself out of debt, how can I start to save, how can I do better financially? The answer to the how is the creation of more financial disciplines, and the why is the purpose as well as the motivation that will get you there! If we did this properly, we would look at it like, Why do I want to win in my finances? Then ask the question. Which disciplines do I need to create to get myself and/or my family there, and then what can I do with the money I have today to get started? More money is not going to fix our problems. Did you catch the language change from "they should," "if only," all the way to "I need to," "I am going to," and "what can I do"? It will help, but by having the right why and building the right disciplines, you will be on your way to win in your finances.

I had a client I was working with, and in the middle of our conversation, I asked her why she wanted to get stable in her finances. After a long pause, she took a deep breath and said the reason why she wanted to get stable is because she never wants her baby girl to ever know what it's like to have to go hungry. If that's not a clear-enough why, I don't know what is! Do you think she is going to let anything stand in her way of making this happen? Not a chance. This momma right here knows her why, and when she is tired and on the edge of burning out, this why will relight that fire, and she will keep fighting to reach her goals! "When you know your why you can endure anyhow."[6]

---

[6] O'Leary, J. *On Fire* (New York: North Star Way, 2016), p. 77.

Breaking Free of Your Comfort Zone

There are many factors to getting motivated and gaining financial discipline. It is important to understand that no matter your income level, building financial disciplines and getting out of debt is difficult. For example, when you have a high income, you generally have a higher standard of living, making it harder to let go of that lifestyle. But when you have a lower income, your amount of disposable income is less, making it harder to make quick progress. We all face different challenges when starting this journey, but no matter your income level, I truly believe you can win in your finances, but you have to be willing to break out of your comfort zone first!

"Comfort is your biggest trap and coming out of your comfort zone is your biggest challenge."[7]

---

[7] Manoj Arora

Higher Incomes

This section, although related to high income earners, is here to show you that anyone can struggle with money, and making more money is not your biggest asset to winning financially!

The higher your income often translates to a higher standard of living and a bigger comfort zone. You find yourself buying more things, dressing up your home, and building a very comfortable life for you and your family. Psychologically, your brain tells you you can afford to keep buying and upgrading as you make a high income and "deserve" it. You should be able to afford another payment. Even when your debt level is rising, you shouldn't need to worry about it; you just need to make more money. You get caught in a cycle of building your comfort zone and using debt to do it. Then even when you do realize that debt is killing your future, unless it is a catastrophic event like a job loss or a death, it is really difficult to break free from your comfort zone and downgrade your lifestyle.

Actors or highly paid athletes are often very susceptible to this. Will Smith is a great example of someone who had fallen into this trap of creating a lifestyle they couldn't afford and having debt hang over their head to the point of near bankruptcy. Here is Will's story.

Will Smith's story

Before Will Smith became a popular TV star on *The Fresh Prince of Bel-Air*, Will made a name for himself by becoming a famous rapper. After landing his first album, he decided to build up his lifestyle by buying luxury. Through all of Will's splurges, he decided not to pay the $2.8 million he owed to the IRS. He slowly started to lose everything he owned. His cars got repossessed, and he was stuck taking the bus wherever he went. It wasn't till Will's lucky break in 1990 where he got an impromptu audition to be the star of the TV show *The Fresh Prince of Bel-Air*. To his surprise, he got the role, but at this point, the broke rapper had lost almost everything he owned, and the IRS was garnishing 70 percent of his wages for the first three years of the show.[8]

Thankfully, unlike a lot of people, Will learned that it doesn't matter how much money you earn, you can still be left broke and in financial ruins. Since then, Will has become a successful actor, and his estimated net worth today is over $350 million. He is one of the highest paid actors in Hollywood.

Unfortunately for a lot of families that do make a decent income, they have not come to the realization that they are actually broke and in big trouble financially.

Here is another story a little closer to home and less Hollywood:

Adam's story

Adam is currently twenty-six years old and grew up in Estevan, Saskatchewan. Estevan is known for its oil and, until recently, was in an economic boom. Adam was doing really well for himself. He was in his early twenties when he owned his own business in the oil field sector and made around $180,000 a year. He had a high lifestyle and was enjoying the wealth by essentially living paycheck to paycheck. He bought a brand-new 2017 Hellcat SRT Go Mango for $95,000, and he traded in his truck that he still owed $15,000 on. This made his payment $1,300 a month in order to keep the vehicle. He didn't know exactly where his money all went, just that he was happy to keep spending it!

Adam carried a debt load of over two hundred thousand in personal debt. Then in 2018/2019, oil hit an all-time low, and being

---

[8] Kozma, L. 2020. https://www.distractify.com/p/how-much-did-will-smith-make-from-fresh-prince.

as that was one of Estevan's biggest industries, a lot of oil businesses either shut their doors or were just hanging on. Adam had to close down the business, and because it was in the middle of the COVID-19 pandemic, he sat on a relief benefit, making $1,400 a month. A big difference between his usual $15,000 a month. He stayed afloat by using credit cards and eventually got a job making $42,000 a year. He surrendered his car and has over $19,000 in credit card debt, one in collections, and the other two soon to follow. When we talked to Adam about his situation, he told us the hardest thing for him to do was to accept the job he did and to surrender the keys to his car. He currently is settling his card in collections and paying off the other two instead of letting them go into collections. Although Adam is still working at getting out of debt, he wants to become financially stable and invest in land so he can build a home for him and his family.

For someone making a high income, getting out of debt is rarely an income problem; it is the size of their comfort zone and lifestyle. The bigger you build your comfort zone, the harder it is to break free from it. It will often take someone making a higher income longer to realize they are in trouble with debt. Therefore, making their journey out of debt take much longer. Your income and lifestyle can keep you comfortable longer, blinding you to the real financial struggles you do have!

Lower Incomes

If you are someone with a lower income, you will still struggle with your comfort zone, just in a different way. People with lower incomes often are just trying to hold on to what is left. The risk seems higher for them as taking any kind of risk can put them and/or their family in a really tough spot financially. So breaking free of their comfort zone can be very scary, and people will often stay in that zone not because it's comfortable but because outside of it is too unknown. The lower-income earners do have a slight edge in this area though because they are closer to the edge of their comfort zones than they think. They are only one or two big emergencies away from having an "I've had it" moment, which will wake them up a lot quicker to their real financial reality.

The more uncomfortable you are, the easier it becomes to break out of your comfort zone. The lower income demographic is also more likely to be able to see their why clearer because of how much closer they are to the edge of their comfort. They haven't built up their lifestyle, making it a little easier to get more uncomfortable where they are. Every emergency they face forces them closer and closer to the edge of their comfort zone. Peter McWilliams was quoted saying, "Comfort zones are most often expanded through discomfort."

Also, once this group does snap through their comfort zones and has an "I've had it" moment, they, in general, are going to fight the hardest to never to go back to where they were. They often work harder and commit themselves to all-in status easier. This is not to dismiss the fact that this group may have an income problem and may need their income raised. However, whatever group you stand in, or if you are somewhere in between, you still need to get crystal clear on your why and change your behavior in order to break the financial cycle you are stuck in. Here are two stories to help illustrate that it is possible with a lower income to win the war on debt. The first story is of a single-income home, and the second story is of a single mom with a fifteen-year-old daughter. Both stories have different challenges faced, but both stories didn't let those challenges get in the way of winning the war on debt.

Lisa and Dan's story

Lisa and Dan were both twenty-five years old when they had had enough with debt and didn't want to live their lives on payments. They had $15,000 in student loan debt and were determined to pay that off in under a year's time. At the time, Dan was still going to school to finish his aviation degree to become a pilot, and Lisa was a stay-at-home mom. They had two kids together both under the age of seven—Timothy, eighteen months; Daisey, four; and Jacob, seven. On top of Dan finishing his degree, he worked full-time delivering pizzas, making around $36,000 a year to provide for his family. They decided that even though it might take Dan longer, they would stop going further into debt for school and, instead, would work to pay off their current student loans even before they came due. With using the income they had and saving money on day care and household expenses, Dan and Lisa were able to live on less than $20,000 a year! That meant that they got out of debt and in just over eleven months, still only making $36,000 a year!

Since they got debt out of their life, Dan finished his degree and has a few job offers to become a full-time pilot! One of the biggest pieces of advice they gave to others in similar situations was don't be afraid to look twenty-plus years in the future; you will realize that a year or two of your life is a small price to pay to make your future dreams come true! Congratulations, Dan and Lisa. You have won the war on debt. Keep going, keep winning!

Gabrielle

Gabrielle was in her early forties (she wouldn't disclose her true age) when she wanted to do something that would change her and Jillian's, her five-year-old kid, life forever. Gabrielle had a student loan for $56,000, a line of credit of $5,000 and a credit card balance of $4,000, all totaling $66,000 in debt. She was able to pay off this amount in under forty-four months' time! When she started this journey, she was working as a registered nurse making $38,000 a year. She vamped up her overtime, and toward the end, she was making just over $70,000 working sixty plus hours/week. Gabrielle won the war on debt and now has slowed her working hours to forty to forty-five hours a week so that she can spend more time with her daughter, Jillian.

When asked what her motivation was to pay off that amount of debt so quickly, she responded that in the beginning stages, she struggled to put food on their table and was trying to do everything herself. She said that she wanted to show her daughter how to be independent by fixing her own mistakes with money, but also to teach her how to know when to ask for help when needed. Gabrielle and her daughter, Jillian, are now saving up to pay cash for a house and starting to save for Jillian's college. Congratulations, Gabrielle. Not only have you won the war on debt but you have changed your family tree. Keep going, keep winning.

Both of these groups have their own struggles, and both have very unique differences. Both groups can break free and win. They just need to know and understand their why. Winning in your finances, and especially conquering debt, is never just an income problem. That is only a small portion. The need to change the behavior is on the front lines.

Nonnegotiables

Give, live, save are the first three disciplines to help you win in your finances. They will keep your family as your top priority and will show you the best path to leaving a legacy for them! These nonnegotiables are not only financial concepts, but much more than that, when you prioritize them in your life, they can and will impact multiple areas of your life as well. We will be looking at these as mainly a financial setting, but also understand they can impact other areas when you start to build them. Each one has transformed my finances and life, and to this day, I keep them as my top three priorities, and I know they can do the same for you. Once you have mastered the first three nonnegotiables and have become debt-free, we will be adding a fourth nonnegotiable. But these three are a great place to start. Each of these steps are put in this order for a reason, and if you want the best chance of you winning, you should treat them this way.

GIVE

No matter what we do in life, there is always a starting point. When doing a three-legged race, starting off on the right foot is key to not falling down before even getting started. We need to think of giving as our first step to getting started, and getting started on the right foot in our financial and life journey. With giving first, there are a lot of benefits when you decide to make it a priority in your life and your budget. Giving softens your heart and transforms you into a more selfless person. Giving creates disciplines and helps you clear clutter from your life that's eating away at your income. Giving also allows you to be part of something bigger than yourself.

When it comes to the financial side, the biggest thing that giving can do is teach you to live on less than you make. Creating that one discipline will help shape your financial future and will set you up to win financially now and for your future!

There are very few people who talk about giving as a financial discipline and even fewer that talk about making it a first priority. Giving, and especially giving first, is counterintuitive and mathematically, I'll admit, doesn't make sense. Giving is the hardest discipline to understand why it works, but if you try it out for at least a few months, you will be given a glimpse of why giving is so important in your life.

The order is more important than the amount!

Before diving in any further, I want to take a moment to help my readers understand that although giving is so important to helping win financially, and create a better future, your income level might make it seemingly impossible to even give 1 percent, let alone the recommended 10 percent. I want to say first and foremost there is no shame in this. Sometimes the money is just truly not there. My first recommendation to you is to just keep reading! There are disciplines throughout this book that can help you get creative and make this giving concept work! My second recommendation is to just start. If you list giving first at 10 percent and you do not get far enough down your budget to cover your basics, it's okay to go back and adjust. Check your other categories of things you can adjust, but ultimately, you may need to lower your giving percent. Even if you end up only being able to give $10/month when you first start, that small step will pay off, if nothing more than helping you see that you can do it! As you pay down debt and find some extra ways to make extra income, you can get to that 10 percent goal!

Another recommendation I have is giving of your time. This recommendation should not replace the other recommendations but should be paired with them. What giving of your time does in these cases is it helps bridge the gap between the effectiveness of giving your full 10 percent financially and what you currently can do. When you give of your time, you are still building effective disciplines like becoming more content, being outward-focused, and being part of something bigger than yourself. As your time is also very limited, you will have to prioritize this style of giving and allow yourself some freedoms when it comes to how much time you can give to the cause. I am a big believer in both giving of your time and your finances, and I do want you to do both side by side, but it may take some smaller steps at first to get to that stage! The one last thing about giving of your time is it can very easily present new opportunities for you in your life that you would have missed out on otherwise!

Giving first strengthens your ability to build the discipline you need to win in all areas of your finance and sets you up for success in the future. One of the biggest hurdles that people have with giving is that they don't have enough when they go through their budget. Most people start by listing out their bills and pay them first, then they go onto household basics like food, shelter, clothing. Then if they get this far, they might set aside a little for savings or giving, not often both. It is highly probable that even if your money stretches to the last two lines of your budget, there isn't much to give… See what I did there? This is why prioritizing your money is so important but also why giving needs to be the first category on your budget. Giving matters, but you can't see the full effects that giving has in your life if you are not willing to make it your first priority. Even if you know you can't make the math work, prioritize giving 10 percent first, then work down your budget. You may still find yourself short, but I know you will make it further down your budget than you did before.

The reason 10 percent matters.

If you are consistently spending 100 percent of your income, you will never get ahead. If you have any debt, it will take you longer to pay off, and it becomes easier to add debt to the pile. I always like to start with a small action step. What if we started living on 90 percent and started giving 10 percent? Did your heart start pounding a little bit harder? Did your blood pressure rise a bit? Good, here's why. Giving 10 percent is significant enough that you can feel the money leave, and it hurts a bit just thinking about it. If you have taken this seriously after your blood pressure rose, you probably started trying to figure out how you could make this happen. What could you cut? Or what is out of priority in your budget? Even though you could feel that 10 percent leave, 10 percent is usually not significant enough that you can't live without it. Robert Morris, the author of *The Blessed Life*, posed the question, "What can you do with 100% that you can't do with 90?"[9] That is a good question we should ask ourselves.

If you are a natural giver, you probably already understand this concept and might even think 10 percent is low. If this is you, I have good news for you. You are further ahead than the rest of us, but there is still a reason why you picked up this book. Maybe you are a strong giver but struggle to put yourself first in your finances. Maybe you are struggling with some debt or can't figure out how to save effectively. The ask I have for you is that you do a thorough calcula-

---

[9] Morris, R. *The Blessed Life*. 2nd ed. (Bloomington: Bethany House, 2002).

tion and force yourself to drop your giving down to 10 percent. It is important to become disciplined in your giving, and you should even try to implement this discipline while getting out of debt. Remember, any small good discipline will have a positive impact on your life now and in the future. Once you reach your financial goals, whether that be getting out of debt or saving for a home, you can raise up your giving rate after, and I encourage it, but we need to create the discipline of being able to say no first!

Giving Affects More Than Just Your Finances

Living on less than you make creates a discipline in your finances that will multiply in all other areas of your life. Living on 90 percent of your income will help you see other possibilities more clearly. When you are willing to sacrifice that initial 10 percent, it kick-starts your giving discipline and shows you that more is possible. This will give you hope and motivation to repeat this process in other areas of your finances. Discipline happens one step at a time, and no discipline is created overnight. Your greatest chance of making a discipline stick is to take one small step at a time. As Mark Twain said, "the secret to getting ahead is getting started."

When we try to "go big or go home," we often go home, especially at the beginning stages of our financial journey. That saying is actually meant for later in life when you want to push yourself to the limit and take the next step. We are not there yet; we are at the learning and growing stages where we need to take small steps to see that small successes are possible. Then those small disciplines created show us the path to success, and we start seeing bigger successes as a cause of it.

When we think of discipline, one of the common comparisons that is talked about is the idea of taking the stairs versus taking an elevator. When we take the stairs, it teaches us how to exercise our muscles both physically and mentally, and trains us to not take shortcuts in life. Instead, we slow down, create one discipline at a time, and understand that life was meant to be taken step by step. When we understand that life started with a single step and that it's okay to carry on at that pace, we will win in the long run. Giving is the first step to creating that mindset and that discipline. Making giving a priority will help you see the possibility and show you the value of living on less than you make.[10]

Giving softens hearts.

For this section of the book, I wanted to share a little bit of my journey with giving and let you all in on a little secret. Giving has never been my strong suit. I would often give out of obligation, but rarely would I give from the heart. When you read my story, I hope you can see that giving not only can change your mindset on situations but can also help you practically navigate and win financially.

When I first started giving, my understanding of giving was very little, but I decided to give it a try. I gave on and off throughout the years, and looking back, I can see patterns of how that affected my daily life. Keep in mind I was not on a budget and had no intention of watching where my money was going. All I knew was there was 10 percent less money coming in on a monthly basis. When I thought this through, I understood that I needed to tighten up on my spending. This meant I stopped going out as much and started spending less when I did. I had no intention of becoming more disciplined with my money. All I knew was I did not want to run out.

I started to notice a pattern in my life when I stopped giving for a season. I saw myself constantly overspending and using my savings and credit card to "not go into debt." I had no feeling of friction with my money as I was living at home and had no real bills, only the lifestyle I chose to lead. This meant no restrictions, and therefore, I did not feel I had to watch what I was spending. The less restrictions I had on my income, the more I felt I could spend, and ultimately, the more I did spend. Giving 10 percent away made me watch my spending habits and made sure I had enough money to make it through each month.

When I finally committed myself to give consistently, I saw my heart soften. God not only blessed me with a raise and a girlfriend

---

[10] Vaden, R. *Take the Stairs* (New York: Perigee, 2013), p. 23.

but also a brand-new car! God also knew I had no patience, so this all happened in one day! Okay, okay, my life did not turn into a feel-good Christian movie. My daily life did not change. I was still single, and my coworker got *my*—okay, their raise. Oh, and I am still waiting for my car to be delivered. Little did I know, something bigger than all that was just around the corner, and in the following few months, I was going to be able to be a part of something bigger than myself. This event not only changed the way I looked at giving but also softened my heart toward people.

At this point in my story, I was giving my 10 percent but still did not have a written budget. I knew I wasn't going into overdraft, and I did not feel a significant difference in my spending habits. The real moment of truth was not until a massive fire broke out in Fort MacMurray. This event was one of the first times in my life I felt I could contribute in a positive way. I reached out to a few friends and ended up taking two groups up to Edmonton, where they had set up supply compounds for the communities that were forced to be evacuated. Without even considering if I had enough money, I was sending out the invites. This terrified me at first, and to be honest, I started hoping that no one would respond to my request. I was unprepared. Having no vacation time left and not knowing where my financial status stood, I was forced to "live on a prayer." The only thing I knew for sure was I had some money and the well was not dry. When I checked my account, which was rare, to my surprise, not only was the well not dry but I had a decent amount of money built up. It turned out I had tightened up my spending habits more than I needed to and ended up creating some margin. There was enough, in fact, that I could pay for all the fuel for both trips as well as any food we needed when we were there.

As I am not the biggest planner, I thought of everything except a place to stay. Thankfully, God had us covered in that area. One of the volunteers at the supply tent asked us where we were staying, to which my friend overheard and "politely" chimed in, making me have to admit I had no plan at all. He offered us a room for the nights we needed it. Then when it was time to head home, we stopped at my uncle's place where we had supper and stayed the night before finishing the drive the next day. My cousin was home and was helping his dad on the farm and heard what we were doing and gave me the keys to his place right in Edmonton. I had not considered asking him for a place to stay as I thought he only rented it for the school year and then lived back home for the summer. This was a huge relief as the second crew I took to Edmonton was a lot larger and probably would have canceled if I would not have found a place.

During both trips, we saw a lot of heartbreak—stories of people losing their homes, their livelihood, and their hope. That fire had burnt down and damaged over 2,400 homes and made another 2,000 unlivable. Because of everything going on, there were very little reports coming in on the whereabouts of the fire, so no one knew which houses had been destroyed. I was talking with this one lady who had mentioned that her house payment was due that day, and she had no idea whether she should pay it or not. The fire was known to be close to the neighborhood where her house was. It had a high probability of being burnt down or, at the very least, unlivable. I could not even begin to imagine her dilemma and all the decisions that came into play in that situation!

We were able to play our part in comforting the evacuees and offering them a little bit of hope. I remember seeing how grateful people were to be given their basics for the next week or so. I spent most of my time in the background, trying to distance myself from the emotions, but the people I talked to and the stories I heard broke my heart, and I knew I was in the right place at the right time. Giving softened my heart.

I would not have gone on those trips if I did not have the extra money in the bank. I would not have had the extra money if I had not made giving my first priority. By giving 10 percent, I created a small discipline of watching where my money was going. That small discipline not only forced me to tighten up and live below my means but also created enough margin where I could say yes to those Fort Mac trips and not go into debt doing it!

I will never forget those trips or the stories I heard. Being able to give up my time and money would not have been possible if I had not created the discipline of making giving a priority in my life. It was during those trips where my heart was softened and I was able to be a part of something bigger than myself.

SCARCITY VERSUS ABUNDANCE

NOT GIVING, OR HOLDING on to everything, keeps you focused on yourself and makes it easier to have a scarcity mindset. A scarcity mindset is the belief that there will never be enough and leads us to say no when we should be saying yes. The opposite of a scarcity mindset is an abundance mindset. An abundant mindset is grounded in the belief that there is more than enough for everyone and makes it easier to say yes when opportunities arise. I understand how easy it is to stay in the scarcity mindset, especially with the life situations to prove it. I truly believe that we start to win when we can find a way to change our mindset. That step is giving. If you can force yourself to let go and give first, you are taking the first step to changing your mindset from scarcity to abundance. Here is a parable by Craig Hill of three rivers and how each family along the river had a different mindset of dealing with it. The first family's mindset was there was never enough, the second family's was just enough, and the third family's was there was more than enough water to go around.

> The first family gathered together one sunny afternoon and determined that their future was at risk. There simply was not enough water to support them. Each day, they watched as the water flowed right by them without stopping and considered it a great loss to their resources. So they built a dam and watched it carefully to make sure no drop of water got through. A large pool of

water developed in front of their house but they continued to live in fear for there was not enough.

This family had a scarcity mindset. They held on tight to what they had in fear of never having enough!

The second family recognized there was enough water for them but only just. They laughed at their foolish neighbours' dam. Instead they used up all the water which the river brought, for what better use could it be put? And was water not designed to be used by them? So little water was left to flow downstream.

This family, although they did not have a scarcity mindset, they did not have an abundance mindset either. They still held on tight to what they were given, but they decided to store up any extra water for their own use instead of believing that they truly had enough to begin with.

The third family looked at water in a completely different way. The third family asked the important question, "How much water is enough?" They understood how much water was available to them and did not use it all. They determined how much was enough for them and used only that amount. The rest of the water was allowed to flow freely downstream to others.

Spring brought new things and the rivers swelled to double their normal size. The first family found it difficult to keep their dam in place allowing some water downstream because they could not contain it all. They took pride in the fact that they were able to share and still keep the reservoir full. The second family was delighted and built a swimming pool for the children and began to water their lawn. They rejoiced in the plenty and enjoyed all kinds of pleasures, still using up all the water so little was left to go downstream. The third family watched their river swell but used no more water than they had before.

One day the third family was out walking together and noticed another village. This village was nowhere near a river and the people had to travel hours simply to have enough to survive. When they returned home and looked at their own river they realized something spectacular. If they built a canal they could supply the entire village with enough drinking water. So they constructed a canal to the village and watched the community begin to thrive. This brought them such joy that they continued to do this for other communities all around them.[11]

The third family had an abundance mindset. Instead of worrying about not having enough, or keeping it all to themselves like the first two families, this family figured out what they needed to live on and even when times were good. Instead of collecting more water, they figured out a way to live life with an open hand and bless others with their excess.

When we start to give, we learn how to be like that third family and start to have an abundance mindset. The more experience we have with giving, the greater our abundance mindset grows. We start to understand that the more we give, the less we need to be content and happy. It all starts with a single step. Give. Giving is the first step you need to take to change your mindset from scarcity to abundance. This is not an overnight process, but if you stick with it, you will see the difference it can make.

---

[11] Enough, M. *Three Rivers: A Money Parable*. 2015. More Than Enough. Available at https://morethanenough.ca/2015/03/20/three-rivers-a-money-parable/. Accessed September 5, 2021.

LEARNING TO THINK BIGGER

GIVING WILL NOT ONLY create discipline and soften your heart but it will also allow you to be part of something bigger than yourself. As a Christian, I believe the church is the hope of the world and therefore the main place I give my time and money to. It is here that it allows me to be a part of something bigger than myself. For others, this discipline might mean giving your 10 percent to your favorite charity or supporting a cause that is making a big impact in your life and others.

Where you decide to put your 10 percent matters. Some charities or not for profits may be taking a ton of unnecessary fees that limit the amount that actually goes toward their causes. If you do not fully understand where your money will be going, become more educated in the charity before you decide if to give. When you don't research and blindly give, you are setting yourself up to stop giving when the first small disagreement occurs. When you do your research, you are less likely to stop giving even when a small disagreement occurs because you have a better grasp of the big picture ahead.

Once you find the charity or cause you want to invest in, you can feel good knowing that your money is being put to good use and is being invested well. The amount of good we could do in the world would be beyond belief if everyone committed to giving their 10 percent first.

We do not live in that world, but we do live in a world where we have lots of charities that have the processes and resources in place that can take your 10 percent and make it go further than you ever

Give. Live. Save.

thought possible. You do not have to give your life savings to be part of something bigger than yourself. Start by making a difference; start with your 10 percent.

Learning To Be Content

Have you ever just looked around and noticed some of the happiest people are the people with the least amount of stuff? On the outside, they look like they have nothing, but they carry a spirit of joy like no other. The more content you are with what you have, the less you compare yourself to others. When we give, our focus comes off of us and onto something else. When we are less focused on ourselves, we start to gain a spirit of contentment. The less self-focused we are, the less stuff we need to be happy. This will also allow us to have a clearer focus on things that matter most. The more content we become, the more we want to clear clutter from our life and start to sell, donate, or get rid of junk.

Comparison

Comparison is the thief of joy. The more we compare, the more we want what others have. The more we compare our lives to others, the more we desire to consume to be more like them. What this does is it changes our mindset from one of contentment to one of envy. When we have a spirit of envy, we are never truly happy. It is difficult to find joy in your life when you are searching for yourself in someone else's life. Convincing yourself to give helps soften your envied spirit by filling it with some positivity. In order to stop a negative thought or a spirit of envy, we have to replace it with a spirit or a thought opposite to it. A giving spirit is a great place to start. When we give, we break the cycles of envy and pay less attention to it. What you focus your mind on eventually consumes who you are. We have to be very intentional about feeding our minds with stuff that will help us change our mindset from an envious one to a more content one, and that starts with giving. "What we feed prospers, what we don't will starve."[12]

The more we compare often translates to the more we complain. When we compare our lives to others and what they have, we start to complain about what we lack. We start to complain about things that used to give us joy! That new car you bought does not smell so new anymore, that house you live in all of a sudden is too small, your clothes don't fit like they used to. Okay, that one may not be a comparison issue; maybe more of a cake issue. It is so easy to fall into the comparison trap and become discontent with our once-perfect life. Instead of telling ourselves the good things we have, we focus on all the negatives. The opposite of comparing is contentment. The more we compare, the less content we become. We need to stop trying to impress people we don't even like and start finding joy in contentment again.

The less content we are, the more we tend to consume. What is worse is we do not consume based on our needs. Instead, we consume based on our wants and wind up with a house full of junk. Consuming with the spirit of discontentment has you consuming to try to become or look like something you are not. We eventually consume so much that we end up creating excess clutter in our lives. The more clutter we create, the harder it is to be or stay content, which just starts the cycle all over again. When our identity is based around our image of ourselves and others, we will never be satisfied.

Giving is such a vital part to breaking all these cycles of discontentment. It is hard to break free of a bad habit. It takes small steps of discipline to change your behavior. That one small step in the right direction is giving since giving is the opposite of comparing, because when we compare, we hold on to a spirit of envy. When we give, we give up a part of that spirit and replace it with something good. Giving softens your heart and makes you a more outwardly focused

---

[12] Craig Groeschel

person, whereas envy hardens your heart and makes you focus solely on yourself. It is not easy to break the spirit of envy or comparison, but all it takes is one step to move forward. Give!

Key points for *Give*:

Order is more important than the amount
- Put giving first on your budget.
- Set your goal to hit 10 percent.
- Give yourself grace; don't give up.
- Give of your time to help build even more discipline.

Why 10 percent matter?
- What can you do with 100 percent that you can't do with 90 percent?
- You can feel 10 percent leave, but 10 percent shouldn't break you.

Scarcity vs. abundant mindset
- A scarcity mindset makes you hold onto all you have.
- An abundant mindset helps you open your eyes to make you see you have more than enough.

Giving allows you to be part of something bigger
- Know where your money is going; where you give your 10 percent matters.
- Give to a place that can do infinitely more with your 10 percent than you could on your own.

Contentment and Comparison
- The more we compare, the less content we become.
- Enjoy *your* life, not someone else's.

LIVE

In this section, we are going to be discussing taking care of your family, making sure they are your top priority, living for the future, and winning the war on debt. When it comes to family, we need to make sure no matter the stage you are on that they are your number one priority. Winning the war on debt, we have to start by understanding the one simple discipline which is focus. When it comes to winning the war on debt, we need to have intense focus on getting that debt out of your life. If you want to win this war, you have to focus on it! Stop investing, stop holding on to that extra money you have under your mattress, stop letting fear make you second-guess your decision to go all in. This is your time to win the war, so get focused. Do these steps one at a time and in order; just follow the process!

Giving first enables you to keep your family as your top priority. Both of these concepts are very important to be prioritized as they are, but I wanted to be upfront that it can seem like a contradiction with how we talk about both these concepts when in fact, they are actually complementary to one another. Giving first is actually a form of making sure your family is your top priority. Giving creates the disciplines you need to making sure your family is and continues to stay your top priority. This does not mean that I want your family to starve because you decided to give 10 percent of your income away instead. We talked about this in giving that even though 10 percent is the most effective, you may have to start your journey with smaller steps. Instead of looking at these concepts using the word *or*, we need to look at them using the word *and*. For example, we could say giving first *and* making sure your family is your top priority instead of giving first *or* making sure your family is your top priority. These concepts go hand in hand, but there's a reason why giving is the first nonnegotiable and why giving is first on the budget; giving creates the disciplines you need to help your family succeed. This is also why I intentionally use different languages when talking about them. I say give first and keep your family as your top priority.

You, your family, others.

Ladies and gentlemen, this is your captain speaking. Should the cabin experience sudden pressure loss, stay calm and listen for instructions from the cabin crew. Oxygen masks will drop down from above your seat. Place the mask over your mouth and nose. If you are traveling with others or with children, make sure that your own mask is on first before helping anyone else.

One thing a lot of people struggle to grasp is the importance of putting themselves first. This is not out of selfish gain or desire; this is out of necessity to make sure you are ready to fight for your family when they need you the most! I want to make it clear that this is not an excuse to neglect your responsibilities or watch your family suffer while you are "putting yourself first." Putting yourself first needs to be met with a specific purpose and needs to be grounded in love. When your needs are met, you stop looking for the world to solve your problems. You are filled up and don't need anybody or anything to fill a void, and instead, you start to give and take action for others, especially those you love, expecting nothing in return.[13]

Choice versus sacrifice.

If you are filled up and your needs are met, then you begin to make choices for you and/or your family instead of making sacrifices for them. When we have the right motive, love, we don't sacrifice, because sacrifice gives us the ability to blame others for our choices. Instead, we choose out of love to make our family our number one

---

[13] Spooner, S. *Your Life* (Bloomington, Indiana, 47403: AuthorHouse, 2012), pp. 29–32.

priority. We choose to put them first and make sure their needs are met before anybody else's are. We choose to work longer hours to get stable or start to get ahead in our finances. We choose not to blame anyone else for our struggles and become accountable to ourselves. Our family is our number one priority, but we can't help our family unless we choose to put on our mask first. We choose; we don't sacrifice.

Your basic nonnegotiables

Your family deserves their basic needs met before you give anyone else your attention. The basics are often called your four walls. I call them your basics. Food, shelter, clothing, and transportation. Food—it is your responsibility to make sure your family is fed. Let me be clear, food doesn't mean eating out every day or having an expensive steak dinner every night. Well, at least it shouldn't. There is a reason why it's called and included in the basic nonnegotiables. Food for your family should be basic. You can loosen this up after you become stable in your finances. Keep your meals simple and cheap! When you make sure you and your family has enough to eat, it will lower yours and your family's stress levels and help you focus on winning in your finances.

Shelter—this is where you get current on your mortgage and all the bills that come with it. The last thing you need to be worrying about is where you are going to sleep or if the power is going to be cut off. This will help keep fear at bay and help unify your family to a common goal.

Clothing and transportation—make sure you have them. Wear some clothes. Bail is more expensive than a T-shirt and jeans. Basic clothing is all you need. Secondhand clothing is okay. Remember it's only for a short period of time. When it comes to transportation, make sure you can get from point A to point B. You do not need a fancy car, you can buy that later. Get something that runs and drives, and take pride in all the imperfections! Make sure your basics give you a solid foundation to fall back on when things don't go as planned!

Budgeting and getting current.

In order to get current on your basic nonnegotiables, you may need to raise your income, cut your lifestyle, or both. With the discipline you created by giving, you will be able to understand it is possible to live on less than you make. It's time to start learning to live simply. This starts with a detailed zero-dollar-based budget. Every month, you need to make every dollar have a name so you can easily see where your money is being spent. Remember, money is a tool and works for you, not the other way around!

Myths about budgeting.

Before we go any further, we need to understand what a budget is and what it is not. There are two types of people—people who hate budgets, and those who love them. This section is for those who hate them. Budgeting gets a bad name because it is seen as a restriction on your finances. This is one of the biggest misconceptions of budgeting. I have worked with a lot of people and have taken lots of time pleading with them to put their spending on paper. The most common response after they commit to trying it out is how far they can actually make their income stretch. I understand there are cases where the income just is not enough to stay afloat. We always have to remember that income is a factor, but even if it is a lack-of-income problem, we have to change the behavior first and foremost. "Budgeting gives you the freedom to spend, but the discipline not to."

Simply writing your expenses down on a piece of paper is a great start. When we write our goals down, we are 42 percent more likely to achieve them. Here is how you set up a simplified budget to set goals for your money. First step, prioritize things that are important to you. Another way you can view them is individual goals you want to succeed at. This is where your nonnegotiables go. Start by putting giving as your first category and then putting a dollar amount next to it.

STEP ONE:

GIVE - 10%	Planned	Remaining
Other Giving	$	-
Other Giving	$	-

Then list your second and third nonnegotiable, live and save and do the same thing. When you put these first on your budget, you are subconsciously telling yourself to keep these a top priority in your life.

STEP TWO:

LIVE - 50%	Planned	Remaining
Food Basics (10%)	$	-
Groceries	$	-
Miscl		
Mortgage & Housing (30%)		
Mortgage/Rent		
Utilities		
Transportation (5%)		
Vehicle Payment		
Fuel		
Maintenance		
Clothing/Misc (5%)		
Basic Clothing		
Miscl.		

STEP THREE:		
SAVE - 10%	Planned	Remaining
emergency fund (1-2 weeks expenses)		

Sinking Funds	Planned	Remaining
1	$ -	$ -
2	$ -	$ -
3	$ -	$ -
4	$ -	$ -

After you list your three nonnegotiables, then go ahead and list your personal nonnegotiables. This is essentially your fun money that helps fuel you as you are trying to get stable. Prioritizing this section is crucial to not becoming burnt out, especially when you are trying to get out of debt. The next chapter, we will be going in depth on nonnegotiables and personal nonnegotiables, but of importance here is that you start prioritizing your budget.

Once you have your personal nonnegotiables listed out, then it is time to prioritize the money left over, from most important to least.

Personal non-negotiables (10%)	Planned	Remaining
1st	$ -	$ -
2nd	$ -	$ -
3rd	$ -	$ -
4th	$ -	$ -
Other Expenses Prioritized		
1st	$ -	$ -
2nd	$ -	$ -
3rd	$ -	$ -
4th	$ -	$ -

Make sure every dollar has an assignment in your budget and you mentally spend your money on everything in your budget before the month begins. What you are doing when you do this is setting individual goals for your income and telling your money where to go; your money needs to work for you. When all your money has an assignment, you will be able to see from your next budget if you overspend, and you can easily figure out where. If you do not have every dollar having an assignment, it is way too easy to spend that money rather than just keep it for the next month.

When you prioritize your spending, it is easier to sacrifice in other areas of your budget. You actually start sacrificing in other areas without realizing it, and even when you do notice it, it does not hurt as much as you thought it would. When we prioritize and set goals for our money, we are more likely to find extra money in our budget and be able to do the things you want to do with it.

Nonnegotiables and Personal Nonnegotiables

There are two types of nonnegotiables. There are your big nonnegotiables. These are things that no matter who you are or your walk of life, it is effective for you to prioritize these things in your life and your budget. If you read the book title, you know the big three nonnegotiables—give, live, save. Then we have personal nonnegotiables. These are things that are specific to your situation, things that fuel you and help prevent you from burning out while trying to get disciplined in your finances.

Nonnegotiables.

Your nonnegotiables should stay as your top priorities in both your financial and personal lives. To help them stay a priority, you need to have them written down. There is no better way to write down personal financial goals than to list them first on your budget. Whenever you make something a priority in the world of personal finance, your budget will be your best accountability partner to tell you if what you spend your money on is actually a priority in your life or not. If you ever wondered what you care about most, a great place to look is your bank account. List the starting three nonnegotiables (give, live, save) at the top of your budget and assign a dollar amount to each of them. For giving, it is recommended that you try 10 percent. Live—this is where you list out your family's basic needs and give each of them a dollar amount. This will differ from family to family, so follow the guidelines listed on the budgeting form (e.g., housing: 30 percent). Now list your third nonnegotiable of save. Save differs depending on where you are in your life, whether you are just starting to get out of debt or whether you are out of debt and just starting your savings journey. Once you have these all listed out and have a dollar amount added to each one, you can move on to your personal nonnegotiables.

Parameters of personal nonnegotiables.

This area can be very easy to overspend in. A good guide to making sure that you do not overspend in this area is to keep it under 10 percent or less of your budget. Later on down the road, you can loosen up on this category. The reason why 10 percent is a good parameter is to keep you focused on winning financially, whether this be getting stable in your finances, paying off debt, or learning how to save. This will keep this discipline your top priority. Personal nonnegotiables give you fuel for energy, help motivate you, and inspire you to achieve your goals quicker. The more you spend in this category, the more it loses its effectiveness. Spending too much in this area will limit your effectiveness and delay your results.

Personal nonnegotiables are where you get your fuel from and will help stop you from burning yourself out mentally or physically. There are huge benefits to finding things that fuel you in life, and it is important to make them a priority. I want to give you permission to enjoy your money, but help you spend and invest it on yourself wisely so that it has a positive rate of return in your life. The example I typically use is going to the gym. We all have that one friend who goes to the gym at least five times a week, and that's all they can seem to talk about. Know a person like that? When they go to the gym, the effects and discipline they create doesn't stay there; it follows them home. It gives them more energy, inspires them to eat better, and in essence, it motivates them to win in other areas of their life. Another example is going out for coffee with friends. For people who crave social interaction, especially extroverts, this will help them recharge their batteries and get them motivated to keep winning in whatever else they do! Both of these examples cost money, but the money they invest in themselves in those areas will pay off by having them recharged and ready to win! It's okay to spend money on yourself. Just make sure it's invested wisely and gives you the proper fuel to keep going and keep winning.

Money is a trade-off.

To help you spend wisely, it is important to understand that every time you spend, you are giving the opportunity to spend in another area of your life. Money is a constant trade-off. If you spend $500 on a pair of shoes, which by the way, I personally can't even imagine what those shoes would look like! You give up the opportunity to use that $500 elsewhere. There is nothing wrong with spending $500 on shoes (although I still want to see these shoes), but when you understand the trade-off, you will find yourself making wiser choices with your money.

Take that $500, and instead of spending it on shoes, put it in the stock market and let it sit for eight years at 10 percent. Your initial investment of $500 now has more than doubled in value! Now let it sit for thirty years, and your investment has now turned into $8,724.70. I don't know about you, but my shoes barely last six months and are worthless by the end of that time. Take another example of instead of spending that $500 on shoes, you instead spend it on a night out with your significant other. The trade-off here is investing into a relationship that could last a lifetime. Or a pair of shoes that, although ironically *did* last longer than my last relationship, will not last a lifetime!

Money holds different values depending on where you are spending it. It also holds different values to different people as we are all unique and driven by different things. Some of us are extroverts and are fueled by having other people around us. So extroverts are more likely to spend money on things like social outings and parties, whereas introverts are more likely to spend their money on books and home comforts. When you understand that money is a trade-off and that you have the freedom to choose how you spend it, you can make wiser choices with it. This will help you spend on things that fuel you in more than one area of your life.

Deserve Versus Earn

We live in a world where we are constantly believing we deserve everything, and we want it without waiting. The truth bomb here is that we actually deserve nothing, even the things we are given. We do not deserve them. When we learn the difference between deserved versus earned, we are less focused on instant gratification and more focused on long-term results.

When we feel we deserve something, it comes from an entitled spirit. The more entitled we are, the easier it is to tell ourselves that we deserve that new car or that new couch and we should not have to wait for it. Marketers and businesses have caught on to this and/or started this and have introduced low monthly payments so you can get what you want when you want it. The attitude sounds something like this: I work hard every day, and I deserve to go out to eat even though it means putting it on a credit card. Whereas when we are not entitled, we are willing to work hard to get something we want. The less entitled you are, the more willing you are to be patient with purchases and wait till there is cash in the bank to pay for it.

When you have an entitled spirit, it is also easier to take credit for what you did not do. The less entitled you are, the easier it is to have an attitude of humility and the more difficult it is to take credit for something you actually did.

When it comes to our finances, we have to take a step back and understand this concept that we do not deserve anything we do not work for. Putting things on payments is the easy way. Take for example a car that you just bought and put it on payments. That car will lose its appeal a lot quicker than if you paid cash and earned it.

When you save up and pay cash for something, you tend to care for it better and take more pride in that purchase. You feel like you earned it, and you did! The more it takes you to earn something, the longer you can stay content with that purchase instead of always looking for an upgrade. We need to change our mindset from what we deserve back to how we can earn it!

To help us change this mindset and create this discipline, we need to create more accountability in our lives. The more accountability we have, the more likely we are to take a second look at our financial decisions. I remember one time a friend of mine called me and shared with me what a big financial mistake they almost made. This couple was almost completely debt-free and had built up a rainy day fund. Their car decided to give out, and the cost of repairs wasn't worth it. So when they were at the mechanics which was conveniently located inside a dealership, they started to look around for a new car. They looked at a new one, one they couldn't afford without putting it on payments. They figured they could "afford" it, but before they bought it, my friend told me that my name and another name was echoing in his head, so they took a step back and ended up buying something they could actually afford. He had that extra layer of accountability. No matter how small it was, it made them take the extra time they needed to make a wiser purchase for them and their family. Get more accountability in your life and we have to change our mindset from a deserved to an earned mindset.

"We have no accountability because we all allow each other to get away with debt, indulgence, and procrastination. We want everything now, and we want it without earning it."[14]

Now that you have set yourself up to understand how to prioritize your money, as well as understanding that money is a trade-off, you are well on your way to succeed! This has all been to prepare you for the financial challenges to come! This is a time where we zone in specifically on the area of debt.

---

[14] Vaden, R. *Take the Stairs* (New York: Perigee, 2013), p. 5.

Winning the War on Debt

After you created your budget and have gotten current on your basic needs, it is time to start making minimum payments on all your debts. This is also the time to save up a small emergency fund of one to two weeks of expenses. This will be covered more in depth in the saving section. But for now, just understand the main purpose is to help you stop using debt and start to use your own money to cover emergencies.

Before jumping into how to deal with your debt, I want to take a moment to help you understand your debt first. When we understand our debt, it is easier to want it out of our lives. The first thing you need to do is to list out your debts. List your minimum payment for each of your debts, including your home, and add them all together. This will show you how much you pay on a monthly basis in debt payments. If this does not scare you enough or you just didn't want to do the math, find a math nerd and walk through these steps with you. Take the interest rate and figure out how much interest you are losing in each of your debts by taking the monthly payment of your debt and multiplying it by your interest rate. For example: $500x.10(10 percent)= $50. Do this for all your debts, and you will find out how much money you are losing just in interest alone. The final step I want you to do is to figure out how much you have left owing on your debts. Once you figure out how much your individual debts total, then combine them all together. When you see your debt piled together and see how much it is costing you in interest each month, you will see your debt as a problem that needs to be solved.

Now that we see you have a bigger problem with debt than what you thought, you have to make sure you follow and remind yourself of your nonnegotiables, especially under live. Make sure your family is your top priority. Food is on the table, mortgage or rent is caught up along with the bills, then transportation and clothing. Once these things are all caught up, continue to make minimum payments on all your current debts, stop using debt, and build up one to two weeks of expenses as an emergency fund. It is time to start winning the war on debt.

Make sure you celebrate all the disciplines you have built as you are going to need those disciplines to win the war. For a lot of you, this will be a long process and one of the hardest financial battles you will face. Now let's get you out of debt! In order to get out of debt, you need to put a plan in place. There are a few different forms of debt stacking, but these two are highly proven methods—the debt avalanche and the debt snowball. I want to take some time to compare these two. This will help you understand them and their effectiveness.

The debt avalanche.

The debt avalanche is where you list your debts from highest interest rate to lowest interest rate, and you pay off the highest rate first regardless of the amount. Once you make it through your first debt, you move down the list.

Mathematically, this system makes the most sense as you are paying less interest over the time it takes to get yourself out of debt. The problem with this method is it does not take into account human behavior outside of the math. As stated multiple times in this book, we need to create discipline in our finances, as finances is about gaining discipline, then working the math. This can also lead to a slower start as it's possible that your largest debt may have the highest interest rate. We need to think above and beyond just the math in order to change our behavior and conquer debt.

The debt snowball.

The next method is called the debt snowball. This is where you list your debts from smallest to largest regardless of interest rates and put all your extra income toward the smallest one first. Whether a debt has 0 percent interest or 30 percent interest, list and pay them from smallest to largest. This method is counterintuitive, and you will need to try it out for your first couple debts to see how valuable it really is. It's not based around math. It is based around getting quick results that keep us focused, motivated, and moving forward. It's about human behavior and not making it make sense with math.

Although both the debt snowball and the debt avalanche are effective ways of winning the war on debt, one reigns supreme. If you run the numbers for both methods, you will see that the debt avalanche, in theory, would win every time, but again, math is only part of the equation. "You need some quick wins in order to stay pumped enough to get out of debt completely."[15]

So although math is important, we need to focus on creating discipline and getting started first. The debt snowball is designed to get you those quick wins, and once those first few wins occur, you start to doubt less, find a little more hope, and tell yourself you can win! Go with the debt snowball. You will find yourself gaining momentum quicker and getting out of debt sooner regardless of the math.

Humans are wired to need to see quick results. Getting out of debt is a marathon, not a sprint. We are just wired that way. But we also need mile markers like in a marathon to show us that we are getting closer to the finish line. The more mile markers we hit, or in this case debts we pay off, the more motivated we are to pay off our debt early. Never underestimate the power of starting by creating small disciplines. "Small wins fuel transformative changes by leveraging tiny advantages into patterns that convince people that bigger achievements are in reach."[16]

---

[15] Ramsey, D. *The Total Money Makeover* (Nashville: Nelson Books, 2013), pp. 104–108.
[16] Charles Duhigg

The quicker we can pay off our first debt, the easier it is to stay motivated and to carry on to the next one. Once you've paid off a few debts, it's easier to feel like you are accomplishing something. Maybe you gain some new inspiration and build some new momentum to keep going. You will become more willing to do whatever it takes to win. You may decide to cut deeper in your lifestyle, work extra hours, start a side hustle, and/or sell everything you can. When you start to see the process start to work, the more inspired you get and the more motivated you become to conquer debt quicker.

There are a few other methods to pay off debt. One more I want to mention though is when you attack your largest debt first. Let's call it the debt mountain. In the debt mountain, you list your debts from largest to smallest regardless of the interest rate and attack the largest one first. The thought behind this one is if you can make it through your largest debt, it makes paying the smaller ones off feel a lot easier. The problem is fewer people can make it through the first debt because it takes longer, and it is difficult to see that they are winning.

One of the reasons why my default method of paying off debt is the debt snowball is because when you start this journey you probably won't have a lot left over at the end of the month to go toward debt. Think of your excess money as the size of a shovel you have. If you have a small shovel and a pile of dirt you have to move, it will take you longer than it would with a shovel twice that size. In fact, most likely, it will take you more than twice as long because of all the extra motions you have to do. A smaller shovel wastes more energy and requires you to take more breaks when you use it. For simple math, let's say you have $100 left over at the end of the month and you have three debts. One debt is $400, another one is $800, and the last one is $3,000. Regardless of the interest rate, which one will you pay off faster with that $100? The $400 debt. If nothing changes, you can pay that one off in four months and then increase your shovel size by eliminating that minimum payment. You haven't built a big enough shovel yet to attack anything other than the little one. Same goes for the level of discipline you have created. You have just started paying off debt. Small steps are required for disciplines to develop to their full potential. Start small and build momentum.

Whatever you do in life, there are always first steps you need to take. If you want to climb a mountain, you do not pick the biggest mountain in your area and just start to climb. You will get a little ways up and just give up. You have to start by learning the basics of climbing first. Then you start with a rock wall and get comfortable with yourself and the equipment. Once you have mastered the small rock wall, you have created enough endurance and knowledge to tackle a bigger challenge. That bigger challenge could be a bigger rock wall or a smaller mountain. The more obstacles you climb and conquer, the more stamina, endurance, knowledge, and discipline it will take to conquer the next biggest one. When you get ready to conquer that big mountain, or in this case mountain of debt, this is the stage where you have increased your chances drastically of being able to make it to the top without quitting halfway through. You can do anything you put your mind to if you take the proper steps to achieving it. Don't worry about the math. Build the discipline and take it one debt at a time—the smallest one first, that is.

How does it feel to be debt-free? The best way I can describe the feeling of becoming debt-free is free. Whenever you owe somebody anything, you are never truly free. Breaking the chains of debt is opening up your world to opportunities you never knew existed. You now have more options, you now can make decisions that are best for you and your family and not controlled by the strings of debt. So breathe that free air, and for goodness' sake, enjoy the freedom!

To help illustrate what it looks like to win the war on debt, I thought it would be fitting to share a real-life story of someone actually doing it. When I heard Justin's story, I immediately knew it needed to be part of this book. Not only did Justin build a lot of financial disciplines really quickly, but he put them into action and ended up paying off $53,000 in debt in under eighteen months making $45,000 a year!

Hello, everyone. My name is Justin. I am twenty-six years old. I am a welder by trade and currently reside just outside Regina, Saskatchewan. When I first started my debt-free journey, I was making $45,000 net income per year, working for a welding shop. I was single at the time and had just built my own cabin to live in and was in renovation mode. I was constantly borrowing money from my parents, to which I did not know the total being owed. I had a line of credit and had just bought a brand-new car five months previous. (I still have that car. It's a Mazda 3, and I love it!) On top of all that, I was taking business classes and was constantly volunteering and giving above and beyond my tithe to my local church.

I always believed I was good with money and that I could just live my life without worrying about finances. I didn't have a budget as my belief was that it would have just held me back from what I actually wanted to do. I was in a hurry to get my cabin finished and did not want to see the amount of money I was spending on it. When I saw that my church was offering a class on finance, I thought it would be a good place to feel good about myself and pat myself on the back for everything I was doing right. I started following the steps being taught and figured out I owed my parents $8,000, I had a line of credit of $12,000, and my new car still had $33,000 left owing on it. All this totaled up to equal $53,000 in debt. I started to look around at some people that I knew were struggling with debt and realized I was heading down the same road. I finished up the life group, filled out a budget, and started putting a game plan together to get debt out of my life.

At this point in my story, I was taking all the overtime I could, but it wasn't enough to get out of debt as quickly as I would have liked, so I took a second job. The cool thing with that second job was it revealed to me how dedicated I was to getting out of debt, so even when the job did not last long, I was willing to keep up the intensity when my main job had some big projects come in that required a ton of overtime, up to twenty hours extra a week. I was paying off around $2,900 a month and, for some reason, wasn't dead or broke. I was about $10,000 away from being debt-free when I was given the opportunity to switch employers which, although was the same pay, had more potential for me to grow. I was hesitant to make the move because it may have resulted in less hours, which would have slowed down my progress. I decided to take the job but took a quick breather to build up some cash in case things didn't work out and to stabilize myself before becoming completely debt-free. I started working and almost instantly got all the overtime I was getting at my old job. This allowed me to pay off that last bit of debt in under four months' time. I was debt-free in eighteen months.

I give God the glory for everything in my life, and I know God played a part in helping me get through my debt. I never plan on going back. I plan to retire early, start my own business, and even pay for my next house with cash! If anyone ever asks me if getting out of debt is easy, I tell them it isn't, but it is 100 percent worth it!

Life Insurance

For this next section, I may come across as preachy or trying to sell you something. I assure you that is not my intent. My intent is to show you how valuable life insurance is and how important it is that you purchase the right type of insurance for you and your family.

I put life insurance as the last point in the live section because I want you to remember that life could be over tomorrow, and all the discipline you have learned and all the progress you have made at paying off debt can come to a screeching halt. This isn't to scare you; this is to protect your family when you're gone and to help you leave a legacy instead of a pile of financial stress.

There are two types of life insurance. There is term insurance and permanent insurance. Term insurance is insurance that expires in a set period of time—for example, thirty years. Permanent insurance lasts for your whole entire life and has an investment component inside of the policy.

Permanent insurance.

Permanent insurance, as stated above, is insurance that lasts your whole life and has a saving/investing component within it. Your monthly premium goes toward three areas: insurance, fees, and investing. So think of this as a water hose trying to fill up two buckets at once. The majority of the water is going to go into the first bucket (insurance), and the rest of the water is either spilled (fees), or is emptied into the second bucket (investments). There are two constants for life insurance. Your insurance bucket will always take the most water, and there will always be spills (fees).

When your policy is first opened, the majority is going toward the first bucket, insurance, and, of course, some of it to spills, the fees. Over time, your monthly premium will start to flow into both the insurance and the investment buckets but will still fill the insurance bucket first. Once the money starts to hit both buckets, your investments start to grow. Your money in investment will start to produce more money. This is also known as the policies cash value. Your investments are likely to make up to 5 percent after all the fees and insurance amounts are covered. After a while, the policy will allow you to loan that money to yourself and use it for whatever you want. Here are a few things to keep in mind if you take this option: This is a loan. It is not free money, and you will be charged interest to pull that money out. The money you pull out will be taxed, and everything you borrow has to be returned before you cash out your policy or pass away.

The older you get, the more the insurance bucket needs your money to stay full, so although your monthly premium stays the same, the policy starts to direct more money back into the insurance side of your account and limits the amount that your investment bucket receives. The less money in the investment bucket, the more your rate of return on your cash value will suffer. Now let's drop one more key piece of information. If you borrow from your cash value and pass away before paying yourself back, your beneficiary will be hit with penalties and will have to put the money back that you borrowed. Then when it is time to cash out your policy because of death, your beneficiary has to choose between the policy coverage amount or the cash value that you built up in it. They rarely, if ever, get both. Permanent insurance has a lot of different names, but the basic setup of them are all the same. Insurance that lasts your lifetime and has a savings/investment component built into the policy.

Term insurance.

Term insurance is simply insurance. Its only goal is to provide you and your family coverage if something were to happen to you within the years you had coverage for. Term insurance is less costly than permanent insurance. This has part to do with the length of the policy but also the less fees you pay when you keep insurance and investing separate. Term insurance will cover you and your family in your working years. It should be in place to replace income, cover debt, and any final expenses. Keep in mind that term insurance is only for a set period of time and does not last your entire life.

"Term insurance is like fire insurance. It pays out the face amount of the policy if the insured dies, just as fire insurance pays out if the insured building burns down. Term insurance is in force for a stipulated amount of time, or term; hence the name."[17]

Here is a diagram using myself as the example to walk you through the pros and cons of both.

| Age: 29 |
| Gender: Male |
| Coverage amount: $250,000 |
| Years needed: 35 |

Term Insurance	Permanent insurance
- A temporary insurance policy with an expiration date. (ex. thirty-five years) - Protects your family from loss of income, enough time to raise kids and pay off debt - Lower payment ($33/month) - No cash value - Can't get benefits unless you pass or are permanently ill	- Lifetime coverage - Ensures final expenses are covered in the policy - High monthly payment ($173/month) - Cash value built up in the policy - Beneficiary receives the cash value or the policy amount, not both

---

[17] Chilton, D. *The Wealthy Barber* (Rocklin: Prima Publishing, 1991), p. 82.

Myths about life insurance.

Before tackling the ins and outs of insurance, we need to understand the myths around life insurance first. The first myth is that you will always need insurance. There will come a time in your life when you will be self-insured. This can occur in two different points of your life: when you are single and have very few liabilities, as well as later on in life when you have no debt and your investments are paying your salary.

First, when you are starting out, you only have to look after yourself. No one else is relying on your income, and you have no debt. Congratulations, you are self-insured. The next stage in your life is where you actually need insurance. You start to need insurance when you buy your first home, get married, or when you start a family. Another big indicator that you need to get insurance is if you are in debt. There is nothing worse than being in a lot of debt and passing that debt onto your family. These years are considered your growing years, and having coverage for these years is important to protect you and your family.

You start to get close to being self-insured once you are out of debt, investing for your future, and getting your house paid off. The big indicator of you becoming self-insured is when your house is fully paid for and your investments have grown large enough that your interest is making the same, if not more than your income each year! At this point, you can either terminate your policy or decide to keep it if you like the extra security it can bring. At this point, you are self-insured and do not need life insurance going forward. You can sit back, relax, and know that you are financially stable!

The next big myth with life insurance is it's too expensive. Your insurance policy is exactly what it says it is—insurance! Insurance will always cost you money. Its purpose is to protect your family financially. This is especially important if your family is reliant on your income—something you unfortunately can't provide once you have passed…or can you? One of life insurance's purposes is to replace an income for those who were reliant on your income when you were alive. This is called income replacement and can give your family a few years of breathing room as they figure what's next for them. To break this myth, we not only need to choose the right type of insurance but we also need to put the numbers into perspective. If you have someone who relies on your income to make it through the month, or have a lot of debt that would be passed to your family, even the higher permanent insurance costing $173 a month is worth a lot more than that $250,000 in coverage. It pays for itself if only by giving you peace of mind for you and your family.

Let's put this into perspective in regard to people's daily spending habits. This may not be you, but it's a good comparison regardless. People spend an average $500 a month on a car payment and call it a need. A study was done in 2018 on how much the average twenty-five to thirty-five-year-old spends on coffee each year. The total came to $2,008 a year or $167.34 a month, and people call it a need. Now I am not telling you not to have your coffee. That would be unwise. I am just helping you put things into perspective.

I only believe in term insurance as if you keep at your financial discipline journey, you will find that at some point down the road, you will become self-insured, and your need for insurance will be no longer. So paying upward of 75 percent more toward your insurance policy for an entire lifetime is unnecessary. Just think what you can do with that extra money.

What to do with the difference.

Whether you switched your insurance from permanent to term or not, think about what an additional $140 a month or $1,680 a year could do for you! If you are still trying to get out of debt, that $140/month goes a long way! If you are building up your emergency fund, think how much faster you can build it with that money. What about investing? What if you took that $140 and put it into the market? Well, let's stop thinking and do the math. Investing $140 a month making 10 percent per year is $1,755.68, making $75.68 in interest alone. Now let's do that for the rest of the policy term of thirty-five years, $475,830.74, which means you made $417,030.74 in interest. This is why it's so important to keep insurance and investments separate!

The problem with keeping insurance and investments together is that it causes more fees to be created within the policy, which ultimately will affect your investment portion or your permanent insurance plan. On average, these investments inside the policy after fees are usually around 5 percent. Here are a few diagrams that will help illustrate the difference between your investments staying separate and the same investments being able to make you 10 percent instead of 5 percent inside the policy. (Assume that $100 a month is going to your investments.)[18]

Figure 1: $100 a month invested at 5 percent

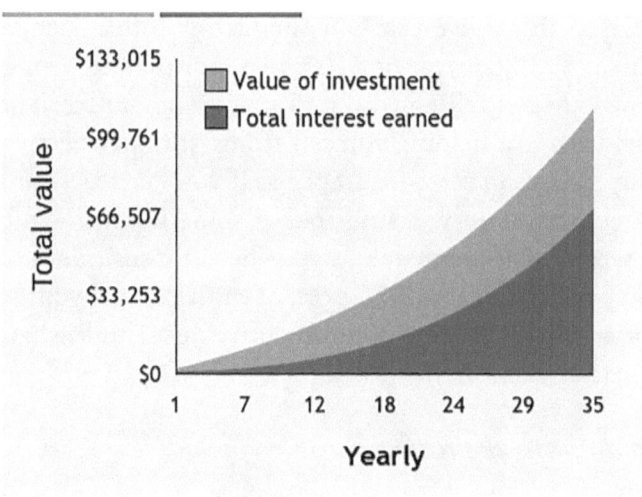

---

[18] This number is a rounded number used to simplify the examples below and should not be taken as an estimated deposit.

Figure 2: $100 a month invested at 10 percent

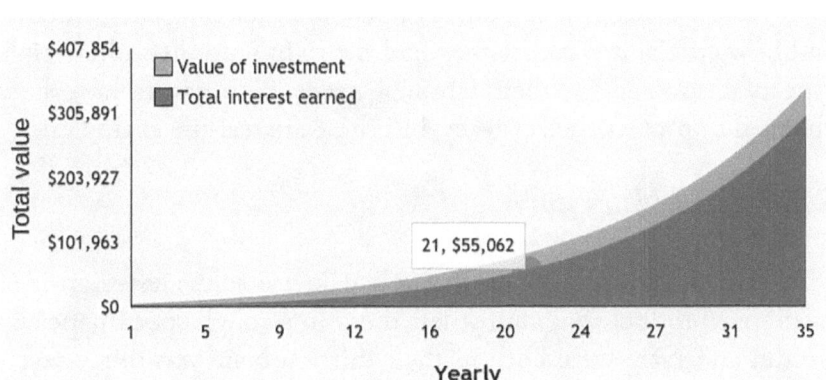

As you can see, in figure 2, the one invested at 10 percent made just shy of $408,000 in thirty-five years of compound interest. In figure 1, it only made $133,000. That means you are missing out on about $175,000. That is well over double! Also keep in mind that this is running on the assumption that your investments in the policy are always making 5 percent and that $100 of your monthly premium is going to your investments consistently. The older the policy gets, the more you pay and the less gets invested. All this being said, keep insurance and investments separate. Your current and future pocketbook will thank you!

Replacing policies?

If you do carry a permanent insurance policy and want to cancel it, be cautious. If you are planning to cancel your insurance, you need other insurance to take its place. Go to a different insurance provider who only sells term insurance and make sure you qualify to get some. Once you qualify and have the policy in your hand, you can go cancel your other policies. The nice thing is, whatever cash value you have built up is yours to keep. Even if you do take a hit with taxes or fees, you can cash it out! So cash out the policies and throw that money at your debt, or get it plugged into some good investments, depending where you are on your journey. Focus on your debt, build a bigger emergency fund and then invest!

Here are a couple of stories of people purchasing life insurance and how crucial it was that they had the right amount and the right type of insurance for their families' needs. The names have been changed to protect their privacy, but these are real-life examples!

Sandra and Nate's story.

Here is a story of a young couple who was sold a less-than-ideal insurance product that almost left them in a tough spot financially. Sandra and Nate were both in their thirties. Nate was thirty-seven, and Sandra was thirty-two. They had two kids, a boy and a girl, and had just got a mortgage on a home worth $300,000 at the time. A life insurance agent approached Nate and Sandra about life insurance, and they ended up buying $100,000 in total coverage, $50,000 on each of them, of universal life insurance, more simply known as a form of permanent insurance. Based on their budget, they could only afford $130 a month for insurance. Sandra and Nate knew this wasn't enough coverage but bought it anyway because it was better than nothing. About a year later, they were approached by another insurance agent and decided to have a sit-down with him to see if they could get more coverage. This agent did a needs analysis on the couple, and with their current debt situation and their want for income replacement, if one of them were to pass, they would need about $400,000 in coverage on each individual. The agent put a term policy together based on these numbers and their budget and was able to get them $800,000 in coverage ($400,000 on each) of thirty-five-year term insurance. They were shocked that the other agent hadn't told them that term insurance was even an option, and ended up canceling their $100,000 in universal life costing them $130 a month and replaced it with their now $800,000 thirty-five-year term insurance for $132 a month. They also decided it would be a wise idea to take an increase in coverage every year so they could get more coverage without having to go through another medical.

A few years went by, and now they had $600,000 each, or $1.2 million in total. Nate was now forty-three, and sadly, Sandra was battling cancer and passed away before her thirty-eighth birthday. Although this is a tragic story, Nate and their two kids were able to pay off their mortgage (now at around $240,000) and their other debts (around $60,000), and because of their benefit increase, they had $300,000 left over to pay for the funeral and to live on.

If Sandra and Nate would have kept their original universal life insurance, Nate and the kids would still have been paying on that mortgage and, because Sandra was the main income earner, would have more than likely piled up more debt just so they could live on. Nate called their insurance agent in tears, thanking them for making sure his kids and himself had the appropriate amount of coverage so that they could celebrate Sandra's life instead of being stressed about how he was going to provide for his two kids. Nate has since increased his policy to $800,000 in coverage and has his kids as the beneficiaries if he were to pass away as well.

William and Rachel's story.

This is a story of a couple who had the right amount of coverage but was holding a mix of term life insurance and whole life.

William and Rachel were both forty-five at the time they decided it was a good idea to get some life insurance. They went to an insurance agent who sold them $450,000 each worth of term insurance and another $150,000 each in whole life, making them have a total of $1.2 million in coverage. This couple was paying around $600 a month to hold these policies. They had both just turned fifty when they were curious about investing but knew they would have to find a more cost-effective insurance to free up some capital to do so. They decided to look at a different company to do investing with. As they were going over the numbers, the agent they were working with told them that they could save $200 a month if they replaced their whole life policy with term. They would get the same amount of coverage and would be able to invest that $200 they saved by doing so. The agent ran some numbers for them at a modest 8 percent growth.

That $200 a month could make them $67,521.26 by the time they were sixty-five! The agent also mentioned that if they didn't need to touch that money till their insurance term was up at age seventy-five, it would turn into $181,798.19.

William and Rachel were pleased with this and decided to go ahead with this plan, and alongside their pension plans, they calculated that they might be able to become self-insured at age sixty, so they wouldn't need insurance and would be able to invest the entire $600 a month into their investments. William and Rachel can now protect their future for today and still invest for their tomorrow!

Here are some final thoughts on life insurance. Life insurance will cost you money, but life insurance will also bring peace to you and your family. The money your family gets from life insurance will not take the pain away from losing you, but it will relieve the stress of money in that situation. It's a way that you can say "I love you" to your family and make sure that they will be okay when you are no longer there.

Key points for *Live*:

Family, top priority
- Put your mask on first; you can't help others without helping yourself first.
- Make sure your family has their basics covered: food, shelter, clothing, transportation.

Budgeting and budgeting myths
- Budgeting does not restrict your spending; it simply sets goals for your money to work for you.
- Prioritize your budget: nonnegotiables first (give, live, save) and personal nonnegotiables (things that fuel you in more than one area of your life), then prioritize the rest.
- Budgeting takes time; don't give up after just doing it for a month; try for a minimum of three.

Personal nonnegotiables
- Keep these under 10 percent of your budget.
- Make sure these are investments and not just wasteful spending.

Deserve versus earned mindset
- We don't deserve anything we have.
- Learn to earn what you buy by not putting things on payments.

Winning the war on debt
- Two different methods of paying down debt: debt avalanche (highest to lowest interest rate) and debt snowball (smallest debt to largest debt); most effective is the snowball.
- You need quick wins to show yourself you are winning the war on debt.
- You need to stop using debt while getting out of debt; have a small emergency fund.
- Getting out of debt is a marathon, not a sprint; you need mile markers inspiring you to keep going.
- What it feels like to be debt free—freedom; you don't owe anyone anything, and you can do anything you want!

Life insurance
- Two types: permanent (lifetime coverage) and term (set period of time); choose term.
- Life insurance is there to protect you and your family from death or permanent injury.
- Can replace your income and/or clear off your debts.
- Life insurance is not intended to be needed for the length of your life.

SAVE

The third nonnegotiable is save. Within save, we will discuss the disciplines of savings in general but then go deeper into each discipline. We will discuss the discipline of using our own money instead of borrowed funds; emergency funds. Creating short-term savings goals, sinking funds, and the art of being able to use your savings to help you save even more in your everyday life!

Saying no to debt

At this point in the process, I have asked a lot from you. You have learned the first two nonnegotiables (give and live), and now we are entering into the third nonnegotiable of save. Although save is a nonnegotiable and a critical part to winning on your financial journey, it is listed last for a reason. When you are giving 10 percent and trying to win the war on debt, savings is the last thing on your mind, at least for me, it was. Similar to giving, you might not be able to save the necessary amount right away; it may take you some time to get there. Start small, and talk in small numbers. Instead of saying, "I want to save $300 this month," instead say, "I am going to save $10 per day." Marketers do this all the time to us; instead of starting with the actual cost of the vehicle, which lets say is $40,000, they tell you it is only $109 per week for seven years. Well, if marketers can do that and have a high success rate at doing it, we need to think that way when it comes to savings. Think in small numbers; your success rate will increase.

At the end of the day, just like we talked about in giving, sometimes, the money just runs out before you can even get started. You will need to get creative; you may need to work some extra hours, do some extra side work, or get really crazy and sell something! The great thing about saving is once you have built up a set amount, especially when it comes to your emergency funds, you no longer need to pour more money into them until you need it for a specific purpose, like an emergency. You can set a goal, reach it, and go back to focusing on paying off debt. Because saving is the last nonnegotiable, you may decide to hang on to that credit card for one more month while you figure out how you are going to get there, and then set small goals to get there. You can do it! You are already committed to the discipline of giving, and that's a monthly investment; saving is just setting one goal at a time, and once you achieve it, you can choose to be done!

In order to win on your financial journey, you have to start saying no to debt. Stop thinking that debt has a place in your life. I have talked to many people who still carry a credit card even though they don't use it for daily purchases. When I ask them why, it often comes back to using it for emergency use. Debt is not a safety net! When we use debt as a safety net, we are telling ourselves that debt is more powerful than our own income. This is why when you are trying to get out of debt, you have you stop using debt altogether.

Debt is not a substitution for an emergency fund. An emergency fund allows you to be free to make big decisions for you and your family, whereas using debt limits the decisions you can make even if you are completely debt-free. Take this common scenario. If you want to move but know it is going to take you a few months to get settled and find a job, debt will play a part in your decision whether you like it or not! Making the move will force you to have to dig back out of debt once you get settled. When you use your own money as an emergency fund, you are able to stay afloat for those months.

The last thing you want is to have a big emergency occur, like a job loss, and have to use debt to stay afloat. No matter how many banks tell you this, debt is not a safety net! You did not work this hard to get out of debt only to be forced to pick the shovel back up and start the process all over again.

To piggyback off of a concept from a previous section about having a scarcity mindset versus an abundance one, debt teaches us to have a scarcity mindset instead of an abundance mindset. A scarcity mindset tells you you do not have enough, and worse than that, it tells you to hold on to what you have tighter. An abundance mindset tells you you are content with what you have and have more than you need. It also opens up your mind to bigger opportunities. The scarcity mindset holds you back from making better decisions for you and your family. It tells you that you cannot afford to quit the job you are in in order to pursue your dreams. It pushes you to either keep you where you are, or forces you to accept less than the best option for your life. An abundance mindset, or the use of non-debt to make big decisions takes the stress of debt off the table and helps you make more clear decisions. You limit your options and your effectiveness when you keep debt as your emergency fund.

Starter emergency fund.

The first emergency fund I want to talk about is the emergency fund you build up before you start paying any extra on debt. This emergency fund's main purpose is to start the process of saving and kick-starting your savings discipline. You will need to build this emergency fund up before you start to win the war on debt. Because you have taken debt off the table, you need this fund there to protect you on your journey. This fund is one to two weeks of your budgeted expenses, just enough to cover small emergencies when they arrive. This emergency fund is especially effective when you are trying to win the war on debt. This amount is enough but also not enough, so it will encourage you and motivate you to want to conquer debt quicker. The faster you can get out of debt, the quicker you get to the step where you can boost that amount up to six months of expenses, giving you more peace in your life and your finances!

For you to really know if these concepts are working in your life, it does take some time, so be patient. It takes about three months to get your monthly budget all figured out, but then after that, it is small tweaks from month to month to keep you going. It takes you about three to six months to see the results of giving first and how that discipline can and does change your life. Be patient. When it comes to paying down your debt, you will find that the first few debts are the hardest to conquer and the easiest to give up on. Keep pushing. The journey may not get any easier, but you will feel like you are winning, which will motivate you to finish!

Here is one of our own personal clients sharing his and his family's stories on how a small starter emergency fund changed the way they looked at money.

Hello, everyone. My name is Collin. Before I jump into my story, I want to tell you a bit about myself. I have a wife and four kids. My wife and I were not on the same page financially. She was a natural saver, and to be completely honest, I thought money was evil, so I would want it to give or spend it as soon as it came in. We had always viewed money differently throughout our marriage, and it caused a lot of tension. Here is my story on how valuable having the right mindset on money and an emergency fund can be.

I did have a desire to learn about finances a bit better, so I reached out to Randy, my legacy coach, and the first lesson I was taught was the importance of saving up an initial $1,000 as an emergency fund. I was skeptical at this process as that is why we have credit cards, right? I decided to give it a try, and it took my family and I four months to build up that $1,000. Keep in mind my wife was the only one working, and we had three kids at the time.

Just after we saved up our $1,000, our car decided to break down and needed all new tires as well as a few other things. I remember stressing out with my wife, wondering how we were going to pay for this bill. I heard my legacy coach's voice in my head, saying, "You have an emergency fund. Use it!" Okay, I didn't actually hear his voice, but after taking a breath, I realized we did plan for this! We had the money to cover it! I walked up to the till and told them to fix the car. My blood pressure and stress dropped instantly, and I went and sat in the waiting room. I actually gave Randy, my legacy coach, a call to tell him what had happened and how amazing it felt to have that money saved up to cover the repairs instead of being stressed and having to use debt to cover it. The funny thing was it took us less than a month to refill that emergency fund. I was all in at this point. I understood that even a small $1,000 emergency fund in place gave me a lot more peace of mind than that credit card lurking in the corner!

The big emergency fund.

After you have created the small discipline of saving your starter emergency fund and are either looking to grow your savings more, or you are out of debt, you are now able to start protecting your life. The first step in this is making sure you do not fall backward by simply not making a plan. It is now time to boost your emergency fund up to six months of your expenses. This will give you enough security to make better decisions for you and your family without having to worry about debt. Once you have the six months built up, I want you to split that fund in half and label one-half as an emergency fund and the other as opportunity fund.

This will give you the freedom to use three months of that fund to take advantage of opportunities that come your way. For example, if your extended family planned a spontaneous vacation and you would love to tag along but did not plan for it, you could use some of that three months and go on that vacation. You can also use this fund to give spontaneously, take advantage of the market, or just simply enjoy it. By putting this fund in your budget, you give yourself permission to use it in any way you see fit and not feel guilty about breaking your budget. You have worked hard throughout your financial journey by saying no, so now it is your time to say yes!

Imagine this: You were offered a job across the country. This is your dream job, everything you have been working for. The pay is a lot better, and the opportunities are endless. The only catch is it is across the country and you have to move you and your family there by the end of the month (three weeks away). The move is going to be costly, and the housing is more expensive, which wouldn't be an issue if you could sell your current home. You know this is the right move for you and your family, but you decided to only build up a three-month emergency fund. You figure out that the three-month emergency fund will cover the move and one month of living expenses but nothing else. You just got out of debt and do not want to go back into it just because of a move. Even though chances are good your house will sell right away and work will start as soon as you get there, you decide to turn down the opportunity because debt is no longer an option.

Now add that extra three-month opportunity fund into this scenario, and it becomes less about a question of money. Your decision is based on if it is the right move for you and your family. Even if you didn't decide to make the move, you will sleep better at night knowing that you made the right decision for your family and not based solely on a financial restraint.

Up to this point, you have been taught and have built multiple disciplines in your finances. You know how to say no, but now you have the ability to say yes. So in volatile or uncertain times, you can label both accounts as emergency funds until things settle down. You can also decide how much security you want in your life. If you want to have more security, you may want to make this a four-month emergency fund and a two-month opportunity fund; this is your choice, but make sure you have six months as a minimum standard. Whenever you decide to use or are forced to use either of these funds, you always want to have them fully funded totaling six months. Whenever you use any of this money, replenish it.

Once your emergency fund is in place, you can take a deep breath. You have built up a ton of financial discipline and stamina. You have a distance of six months between you and debt. If nothing else, that is a great feeling! Now if a job loss or other big emergency occurs, you have up to six months to find a new job or six months of money to pay for an emergency. I had a season in my life where I was constantly jumping from job to job. Not because I wanted to but because I had to. My first job, I got laid off because of it being seasonal. I only had about $1,500 to live on for the next two months before my EI kicked in. During that time, I was constantly looking and trying to find work. I eventually gave up looking for a job I wanted and had to settle for a job I needed. I did not have anywhere close to the money I needed to stay afloat. After about eight months, I quit that job and started the next one a week later. The next job laid me off after three months, and once again, I had not planned for it, so I was stuck taking another job I did not want.

At this point, I did what most people do. I got a line of credit as a "safety net." That safety net only lasted until the interest jumped to 15 percent. At this point, I realized if I did anything different, I was going to save up and have an emergency fund in place that did not carry any interest! The rest of my story followed shortly after, but I learned an important first lesson: debt is not an emergency!

Saving with the Future in Mind

Sinking funds.

Saving not only protects your future; it also helps you plan for it. Sinking funds are a great approach to planning for future needs and upcoming expenses. A sinking fund is a set amount of money you put away every month to save up for a big expense or a larger purchase. There are two types of sinking funds. The first type is for bigger expenses. These expenses could range from car insurance, property taxes, or any major holiday. Whenever you know you are going to have an expense that is not a monthly expense, you can use a sinking fund to prepare for it. If your car insurance costs you $1,500 a year and comes due every year, you can save a little bit each month to pay for it. For that example, it would be $125 a month that you list in your budget, giving it the name of sinking fund/car insurance. When the time comes to pay that bill, you will have saved up that $1,500 to cover it. You can do this with just about any expense that is not a typical monthly expense. One of the more common sinking funds for expenses is your property tax.

The next sinking fund is for future purchases. These are things like purchasing a newer car, saving up for a vacation, or saving up for a down payment on a house. The same concepts apply. You take a look at your time horizon, how much you need to save and by when and then plan accordingly. The key to making sure you do not spend this money elsewhere is to clearly label it and put it in your budget so you know it has a purpose and should not be spent.

When we create sinking funds, we are protecting ourselves from falling into the payment trap. Making payments on things used to be only for big purchases like houses and land, possibly a vehicle. In the past years, society has shifted and has allowed you to put everything on payments. Now instead of just your house, your land, and your vehicle, you can make payments on your fridge, your TV, your bed, your dog, and everything in between. Here is what happens when you start putting things on payments rather than paying cash.

Payments versus cash.

When we pay out of our own cash, we end up spending less because we are focused on our needs and not our wants. When we put it on payments, it is a lot easier to make it more about our wants, which in turn costs us more money. We think twice when we have to drain our bank account to make a purchase. We take some extra days deciding on whether the purchase itself is worth it, and we are less willing to give into all the extras. You are more likely to say, "We do not need that," when you pay cash. It makes it more difficult to impulse buy when you see the full price tag and not just the "low payment" sticker.

Stop the payments.

Don't fall into the payment trap. When we put things on payments, it makes us feel that we can afford more, and we tell ourselves that it is only a couple extra dollars per month. When we take this philosophy, we start adding extras into the purchase. If the cost of the item is $200 a month and the next model up is only an extra $20/month, it makes it extremely painless to upgrade. It pushes you to want to get something you think you need instead of just being focused on what you actually need. Payments cause us to think that we can afford something better instead of what our bank account actually says. The way things are marketed to us, it makes us shift our mindset from "we want a new car" to "we need a new car," with 110 extra useless expensive features added in that we will never use.

But to be fair, they are cool to look at… What we used to think of as a want, the stores market to us as our needs, and we all fall for it, and if our bank account says we can't afford it, the low payment option says we can! We actually have very few real needs in life. Most of our purchases are wants.

Why cash?

Paying with cash helps separate your wants from our needs. When we separate these two worlds, we end up spending less. When we have a better understanding of what our needs actually are, we identify our needs as needs and our wants as wants, but both are limited by what's in the bank. When we limit ourselves to the money we have in the bank, we spend less because we focus more on our need for that item and are less likely to get as distracted with our wants. It will help you spend less!

Our spending habits need to cause us a little friction in our life. The less friction there is in the purchasing process, the easier it is to overspend. In an article written in *Forbes* magazine, there was a study done where two groups of people were given the ability to purchase basketball tickets. One group was told they could pay with a credit card, and the other group was cash only. The group that was told they could pay with a card were willing to pay twice as much as those with cash.[19] In another study done by the same group, they found that people often paid up to 100 percent more on everyday transactions when they used their credit card versus cash. If you were like me, you might be saying, "Well, that's not me. I don't fall for those marketing gimmicks, and I for sure don't spend 100 percent more on daily expenses!" You might be right. This may not be you, but what if you even spent 20 percent more or even 10 percent? Wouldn't it be worth keeping your credit cards at home to save even 10 percent? I want to set you up on a challenge. Choose one item in your budget,

---

[19] Hardekopf, B. *Do People Really Spend More with Credit Cards? Forbes.* 2018. Available at https://www.forbes.com/sites/billhardekopf/2018/07/16/do-people-really-spend-more-with-credit-cards/?sh=12f121c11c19. Accessed September 5, 2021.

and only use cash for it. Mine is groceries. At the beginning of the month, I pull out my set amount for that category in cash and I limit myself to only spend that amount in the category. After you do this for three months straight, compare your three months using cash to three months without using cash. You are likely to see a difference. Maybe not 100 percent difference, but still a difference! My rule of thumb is if you are going to keep a credit card around, do not use it as an emergency fund, and only use it for automatic payments like your power bill. When you go out shopping, keep it at home. Your budget will thank you!

When we save money, we are essentially saying no to debt. Having even a small emergency fund of one to two weeks of expenses can bring you peace of mind and help you cover those small emergencies that arise. Whether you are still in debt or are debt-free, being reliant on your own money gives you more security and confidence than any credit card will no matter what they tell you! Whenever you can create some sinking funds, these will help you plan for the future and not be surprised when your car insurance comes due or Christmas arrives! And lastly but certainly not least, stop giving other people your money in interest. We already lose enough in taxes. Spend with the cash you have in the bank, and you will become much more focused on your actual needs and not overspend on your wants! Savings not only protects your life today but it also helps you plan for the future!

Key points for *Save*:

While getting out of debt
- Stop using debt as an emergency fund!
- Build up a small emergency fund of one to two weeks of your expenses.

The bigger emergency fund
- Build up six months of expenses once out of debt, or when times are tough.
- Split that fund into two categories: three months emergency, three months opportunity.

- Having a large stockpile allows you to take advantage of situations and allows you to make better decisions.
- This emergency fund allows you to say yes.

Saving with the future in mind
- Sinking funds are a great way to plan for big expenses that happen every year and helps you save money.
- Sinking funds fall into two categories: future expenses and future purchases.

Payments versus cash
- Every time you put something on payments, you are more likely to spend based on your wants instead of your needs. You ultimately spend more.
- When you spend with the cash you have in the bank, you will feel the friction of your money leaving and be more tempted to say no to the extras and truly buy what you need.

Conclusion

Congratulations, you have walked through the first three disciplines you need to win in your finances and in your life. If you haven't already, this is your chance to get started. When you start by giving, you are taking your first step to changing your finances forever. Living on less than you make is such a crucial starting point as that discipline grows in other areas of your finances as well. Above that, you will start to change your perspective on leading your life with open hands instead of holding on to everything closefisted. You stop comparing as much and become more content with what you have. It may be countercultural, but it will change your life. Live—your family is your top priority. Prioritize your life and your spending, and you will not only win the war on debt but you will be building a solid foundation for your family's future. It's time to stop using debt and start using your own money to protect your family and save for the near future.

I hope this book has helped you build financial disciplines and helped you find hope in your finances again. Keep going, keep winning.

My Support System

Although it wasn't until recently when I figured these financial concepts out, I can now look back and see that my parents were the ones who actually taught me these concepts. I was just too smart to listen. My parents from day one taught us kids the importance of giving and making sure it was a priority in our lives. They made sure that family was their top priority and that us kids had more than enough to eat and were cared for. They also kept savings a priority even though there was very little left over. I may have been woken up financially by other people and other authors, but when I was interviewing my parents, it's easy to see where it all started.

Charlie (my dad) is a pastor at a church just outside Estevan and has been pastoring there for over eighteen years now. If you know anything about pastors, you know it has to be a calling as most of them do not get paid anywhere near the amount for the time that they put in. He is a father of three boys and is married to Darlene (my mom). If you ever met him, you would probably say something like he is very soft-spoken and has a very calming presence. Here are a few questions I asked him in the interview.

1. Who taught you about finances, and what did they teach you?
    My dad was my biggest influence when it came to teaching me about finances. There were three big disciplines he taught us: tithing, don't waste money, and don't spend more than what you have. I remember one of the first lessons he taught me was he would give me money on Sunday to put into the offering basket. Tithing was always

my dad's first priority, and even when you don't have a lot, your first 10 percent goes to God.

My dad was also never one to waste money. When he would give us money to spend, if we foolishly spent it, it was communicated to us. He was very watchful when it came to money and made sure himself and us were spending it wisely, except at Christmas. I remember him being extra generous at Christmas and giving generous gifts to us as kids even though we were poor.

One funny story about my parents in their later years was when their TV broke, and it couldn't be fixed. The cost of a nice new one at the time was going to be $800, and the TV guy brought one to their house for them to try out. But this was too much in my dad's mind, and he didn't want to spend it. My mom went into her room and came out with a large stack of $20 bills and started counting out the $800 on the table. I guess the TV was worth it to her, and my dad had no idea she had that much cash lying around!

My dad was never a believer in debt. His philosophy was you never spend more than what you have. I was four years old when my dad had to sell his farm and move into town. We didn't have a lot of money, but the farm wasn't making money. He worked hard to put food on the table for us and did what he had to do to not go into debt. Debt was not an option, not even the house. I am thankful to my dad for what he taught us, as we would have not gotten through the early years of my ministry without it!

2. What are some of your beliefs on finances?

My beliefs on finances followed similar to my dad's beliefs. Put God first with your tithe, and live on less than you make. I believe that everything belongs to God, and if we are good stewards with what he has given us, he will provide for our needs. I have tried to give to the church and even when times were beyond tight, God provided for me and my family. As a Christian, I believe that God has set the tithe (10 percent) as the minimum standard for all his people.

The second belief I have is to live on less than you make, and that means no debt. Debt was never an option growing up for me, and so when God called me into ministry, I was determined to go through college debt-free. I worked hard throughout the summer and got as many scholarships as I could. In the end, I was able to complete my degree with next to nothing in the bank, but completely debt-free.

3. What are a few mistakes you have made over the years?

One mistake that I made, especially looking back, was not tithing throughout college. Knowing what giving and tithing has done in my life, I believe that was a mistake not to. I have seen so many blessings from giving, and throughout the years, we have estimated that now we give about one-third of our income away. I believe that 10 percent, or the tithe, is just the starting point.

Another mistake I made financially speaking was trading in for a new vehicle. We had a good running vehicle, but my want for something better got the best of me. I have since noticed whenever I bought a new vehicle, I got too attached to it. I was concerned about loaning it out of fear of it getting scratched, dented, etc. Even if I could, I don't think I'll ever buy a new vehicle again.

4. What is some advice you would give to others?
Have realistic expectations:

You don't always need to buy high-end. Stay within your means; stay content. When we were looking to buy our retirement home, we took a look at our budget and thought that $250,000 was reasonable. There were definitely better houses with more of our wants, but we stuck with that number as it was going to fit our needs. We had put in an offer of this amount, hoping the owner would take it. The previous owner countered, and as it was above the number that we had talked about, we decided to hold firm. After thinking we had lost the house, the owner agreed to our offer, and we kept it in our budgeted amount. Live within your means. Don't overspend based on your wants.

Avoid monthly payments:

Whenever you can avoid paying payments, especially for debt, specifically vehicle debt, they lose their value so quickly. If you are going to buy something, save up and pay cash for it. If you have bills like your car insurance, pay it for the full year. You will save yourself some money.

Marry a generous wife:

Marrying a generous wife has made me become a more generous person. Whenever Darlene and I felt we should give to something besides our local church, we would sit down with one another and talk through what we wanted to give. More often than not, her number was higher or even twice as much as mine, and we would usually agree to compromise. I wouldn't be anywhere close to as generous as I am today if Darlene didn't have the spirit of generosity that she does. We are now giving one-third of our income away in many different areas, and she would still love to give more.

Closing thoughts:

Without God in control of our lives, we would have never been able to do what we have done. He has not only met our needs but exceeded our expectations. Our story as a pastor and wife is to give everything you have to God with no expectations, and he will provide for everything you need. Whether it's financially, emotionally, or physically, God provides. Give back to God, live within your means, and God will carry you through!

After I interviewed Charlie (my dad), I wanted Darlene (my mom) to share her journey on how they were able to make it through all those years and not go into debt. I don't ever remember either of my parents complaining about their situations, and for my mom's case, it maybe had something to do with the fact that she had three hungry kids she had to look after. If you ever meet my mom, you would see a strong work ethic and a desire to help you in any way that she can. This is her story on how they made it through all those years!

Darlene (Mom)

Money is something we have had to learn to be wise with since we have never had a lot. Choosing to be content, spending only what we had, and being willing to take jobs as opportunities arose were common themes. Our family adopted the attitude that we would be generous to our neighbors that were in need and to people in developing countries with whatever resources God gave us. The following explains how we tried to make our money work for us.

I learned how to budget and give from my parents. They paid us to work on the family farm. Well, that was the theory! Teens use way more energy getting out of work than the actual work required, so I know it was a headache for them. But out of those wages and a yearly 4-H calf, we were expected to buy our own clothes and some other routine things. It would have been way easier to just give an allowance and have Mom and Dad buy our stuff, but the lessons would not have been learned.

That same process was used to teach our kids money management. Each kid had a pet and was responsible for them. It was a constant struggle to get dogs walked and fish fed by the kids and not parents, but worth it. Work was to care for their pet and household chores and work got paid. That money was expected to care for some clothes and eating out (responsibilities were appropriate for their age and changed as they got older). Everyone learned that things come with a cost. One time, we were eating out, and one son had spent rather foolishly earlier in the month and didn't have enough money for french fries. There is a bike story that floats around our family of selling a bike to a brother without the seat because he couldn't afford the full asking price.

When Charlie and I had three babies in just over thirteen months and took a large pay cut on an already-small paycheck, we had to do some assessing. I was already home, so I took in a couple extra kids. At one point, I chose to drive a school bus. I didn't have kids, so someone else could be their mom, and it made more sense for me to be home and save money rather than spend gas money and pay babysitting costs. We have taken less desirable jobs and lower pay sometimes just because it is better to be working and looking for something else than not to be working at all.

There is a posture of contentment that is necessary. Almost nothing was bought new. Why would we? At a fraction of the price, you can often find very good used clothes, shoes, toys, and household items. There was a time when fabric was cheaper, so I chose to make most of our clothes. Homemade clothes don't work when kids decide it isn't cool, but by then, they were already buying their own clothes and bought what they wanted, and it seemed they took better care of them. One Christmas, the guys all picked out their own Western material and made their own Western shirts. Great memories and perfect time to spend together as mommy and son. Lots of clothes are destined to be thrown but still have parts that are useful for patch quilts. Every couple years, each boy got his own blanket. You might think that some of this stuff is old-school and not cool, but I noticed that a couple of those blankets are still being used years later on the guys' own beds.

As you can imagine, the grocery bill for three growing healthy boys was rather hefty. Until recently, our property always had a garden, and it yielded lots of potatoes and veggies. If you don't count your time, that can be very cost-effective. Also, choosing foods at the store that actually require you to cook them is cheaper than processed foods. Cooking one meal a week was one of the chores required when the kids were at home. Some turned out to be great cooks, and one still insists that vanilla works with mac 'n' cheese!

When making a choice on how to spend, it was always a question of, how important is it? Do we really need satellite TV, or extra data? How about the expensive dress, or is the cheaper one okay? Does the car need to be new or just something reliable? Holidays don't always have to be at a resort that is expensive; camping can be just as relaxing. If we didn't have the money, we just didn't spend it!

Sports will eat up a lot of valuable family time and money. Especially hockey! So as parents, we made a decision (parents are responsible to make good decisions for children even if kids don't agree with the outcome) not to include hockey. It was expensive, required Sundays, and there was way too much competition and running. There were other things we allowed that were more suitable for us, so each kid was encouraged to be involved in one thing after school.

Long before ketchup was invented, the government used to give a baby bonus (it has a different name now). That was gift money in our eyes, and it was set aside for family vacations that were major trips every few years. Seems important that we understand how easy life is in Canada and to help remember that we spent time helping less fortunate people in Haiti and visited my sister's family in the Philippines. God abundantly blessed us. Like a plane engine on fire that took us back to Seattle, which meant we missed our flight in Hawaii. The airline paid for a huge suite and food for the first night, and we even got bumped again the next day! Two days in Hawaii almost cost-free! Celebrate those times when they come! But when you see an orphan girl whose leg has been chewed by a rat, you come home with a different attitude about life in Canada. It was a good spend of the baby bonus.

Somehow, God always gave us enough for our family and more. We don't remember all the kids that spent days and sometimes weeks at our house because there was a need. Blessed to be a blessing. Using what God has given to help others never is wrong. We used what we had available at the time, only spent what we had, and chose to be content. Are we rich? You bet! Maybe not with money, but we live comfortably. Rich in a family that is tight and enjoys life and each other, rich in memories, rich in relationships with people, and rich because we know God personally? Yep! We have peace and love life.

Ours is simple and fairly uncluttered. We are blessed and choose to bless others with what we have.

My response

My parents have always provided for us kids, and hearing all the specifics of their financial situation, I don't know how they did it! I knew my parents drove the school bus for some extra income, but I was shocked to learn that they didn't spend the majority of it. Instead, they started investing for us to go to college and a little bit for their retirement. My parents were never after financial success. Their priority was to God and their family. The subject of money was never a hush topic in the house, but I have never heard my parents complain about their financial situations. They taught us well (whether we listened or not). It took me twenty-seven years to finally see the value of what they taught me. I remember my parents giving each kid $500 to put toward a car. We could buy whatever we wanted, but they would only give $500 and we would have to supply the rest. I myself, being the perfect/favorite child, would never complain about only getting $500 as all the other kids' parents were giving much more. I would never do that. I also remember my dad saying that even if he could have paid for all of our schooling, he wouldn't have. And again, the perfect child would never think to himself that it was a cop-out answer to not have funded the whole thing. I do remember having these thoughts in both of these situations, but looking back, I wouldn't have done anything different, and I am grateful that my parents taught me the value of earning everything you have, and just because something is given to you doesn't mean you deserved it; it is simply a gift. One thing that shocked me the most about their story is that they are giving over one-third of their income, and trust me when I say this: pastors are underpaid, and even decently paid pastors do not make a lot of money. I am grateful for everything my parents have taught me and continue to teach me with their generosity, and I hope I will not only pass it on to my future kids but also to a whole ton of strangers!

INVEST

CONGRATULATIONS, YOU ARE MASTERING the first three nonnegotiables! At this point, you have not only seen the value in each of the disciplines you've created but are wanting to push the envelope and take another step forward. At this point, you should be consumer debt-free and have your six-month emergency fund in place! Take some time, go out and celebrate. You have been preparing for this next step all along. You maybe just didn't know it! Your journey has not been easy, but it has been so rewarding. It's time to start to prosper in your finances and plan for your future. It is time to add to your nonnegotiables. So far in your journey, you have continuously given, which created the discipline of living on less than you make. You made sure your family was your top priority. You have made savings a priority in your life by protecting your life now but also creating short-term goals for the future. Now it's time to think long-term. Now it's time to invest!

Saving versus investing

Investing is the first step in your life after debt. Before getting into what exactly investing is and why it is so important, I want to distinguish investing and the nonnegotiable of saving. In general terms, savings is anything five years or less, and investing is anything five years or more. These time horizons are important because with savings, you need your money to be easily liquid (accessible). When you are saving money, you are not looking for a lot of growth on this money. Money needs to have a safe place to sit and wait but be ready to be used at any point and time! The shorter your time horizon of what you are saving for is, the more liquid you want your money to be. If you are saving up for a vacation six months away, you will want your money 100 percent fee-free to pull it out. If you are saving up for a house down payment and are projected to take five years to get there, put some money in a moderately conservative savings plan and make a little extra on it. The big picture here is not to treat your savings account as an investment account. Keep your money liquid and not locked in and volatile.

Invest

When it comes to investing, investing is for five years or greater because your money needs time to compound and grow. Your investment money does not need to be liquid and should in fact be locked in to let compound interest take over. The shorter you have to invest, the less time your money has to grow and multiply. Unlike savings, your money should be making you money, not just sitting and making a low rate of return. Investments, like savings, have a specific purpose to achieve. The differences are the rates of return and time horizon. Savings is under five years with a low to no rate of return, while investing is greater than five years with more aggressive rates of return. Think about things like retirement, your kids' college, or real estate investment. These are all things that are down the road in your journey and have time to wait. Your rate of return on investments should be 9 percent or above. Investments can be volatile, but let them sit long enough, and your money will make you more money than you could ever do on your own. Invest for long-term growth. Save for short-term needs and wants.

Investments and debt

The reason why investing is not included with the first three nonnegotiables is because you should not be investing while you are still fighting the war on debt. Your investment journey starts when you become consumer debt-free. Not only will this push you to get out of debt quicker but it will maximize your return on investment

(ROI). When you are debt-free and can put the majority of your attention to investing, you can win big.

Don't invest with debt. Investing while in debt is a bad idea. We established when talking about getting out of debt how you need to focus on one thing at a time to win. The reason why you focus solely on paying off debt and stop all investing was so that you could get through your debt quicker. Master one discipline at a time! The quicker you get through your debt, the quicker you can build your emergency fund, the more effective you can be with your investing. When you focus on one step at a time, you find yourself being more effective in whatever discipline you are trying to build. The less you have to multitask, the more effective you will be. So be patient, win the war on debt, build your emergency fund, then start investing for your future.

Rates of return

One of the biggest arguments I get is people telling me they get a match from their company, so they do not want to give up free money. I understand this urge, as I was very reluctant myself not to take my company's match. At the end of the day, it comes down to motivation. Cutting back can give us a fighting spirit. The more we have to cut out of our lives to win, the more determined we become to get to the finish line quicker. Cutting back looks different for everyone, but if you use those cutbacks to your advantage, it pushes you to win; remember getting out of debt is a marathon, not a sprint. The more you cut, the more fuel you create to get to the next mile marker, and ultimately, the quicker you can get back to investing.

Are you ready?

When you invest using debt products, you raise your risk level and you sacrifice your return on investment. Say you have a line of credit that holds a 5 percent interest rate on it, and you invest into the stock market and you get a 10 percent rate of return. You made 5 percent. The problem is you actually only made 2 percent. Inflation rises an average of 3 percent a year. What that 5 percent got you last year will only get you 2 percent this year. Your real rate of return after inflation is only 2 percent, and you carry a lot more risk for it. If the stock market fell the next year and you made 5 percent or less, your net profit is below zero, and you still carry the same risk. Now if you took that same math and waited till you were out of debt, you could make 10 percent, 7 percent after inflation, or a down year at 5 percent and still come out ahead with 2 percent. When you do not use debt to invest with, you lower your risk, and you get your full rate of return.

Debt and risk

Debt always carries risk. No matter what debt you have, there is always risk involved. The more debt you carry, the more risk you accept. It is easy to measure rates of return but harder to measure risk. The less control you have on your money, the more risk you accept because of it. One hundred percent of debt can be recalled, whether it is a mortgage, car, furniture, or a dog. When you do not own what you have, the actual owner can come at any point and take it away from you. That risk can be exposed with a job loss or a bad business deal. In a blink of an eye, you can lose everything you worked so hard to get and wind up with less than nothing. Being debt-free and having an emergency fund is the best protection from financial risk you could have. Once you stop using debt on anything, your risk level drops.

How much should I invest?

The general rule of thumb for a beginner investor is 10 percent. This 10 percent should be added to your budget every single month after the nonnegotiable of save. So your budget should look like this: 10 percent giving, family needs, save and then 10 percent investing. If you consistently do all four of these before anything else, you will achieve success in your finances and your future.

Give. Live. Save.

Investing tips

This is where I share the secret sauce of what I invest in and how you can be a millionaire in a day. Catchy clickbait, but no, there is nothing secret to what I am going to tell you. Here, we will go into investment options and share some advice that will help you win no matter what you are investing in: invest as early as possible; know and understand what you are investing in; diversify your investments; be frequent and consistent in the market.

Investing early

What is compound interest? Well, let's start by showing what traditional interest is and then compare. Traditional interest works like this: You invest $1,000 and it makes 10 percent or $100, so your total is now $1,100. If you make the same percent next year, you make another $100, making your total $1,200. Keep doing this for a few years, and you will get $1,300, $1,400, $1,500, $1,600, and so on. Let it sit for forty years, that $1,000 turns into $5,000. Not a great return for having your money sit for forty years. Now compare that to compound interest.

How compound interest works is if you put in $1,000 as your initial investment and it makes 10 percent, that 10 percent makes you $100. That $100 gets added to your initial investment, making it $1,100. That $1,100 gets invested and makes another 10 percent. That 10 percent is not just on the initial investment but also on that $100 you made in interest last time, making your total $1,210. Do this again for the next few years, you get $1,331, $1,464.10, $1,610.51, $1,771.56, $1,948.72, and so on. Over forty years, that initial $1,000 turns into $45,259.26. That is a pretty good return for just starting with $1,000 and much better than that $5,000 with traditional interest! The earlier you can start investing and let compound interest grow your money, the greater your investments become. Albert Einstein was quoted saying, "Compound interest is the eighth wonder of the world…he who understands it earns it, he who doesn't pays it."

Because of the magic of compound interest, your 10 percent of your income can turn into millions for when you retire. Don't believe me? Watch this: If you make $48,000 a year, that means you are making $4,000 a month, which means you should be investing $400 a month or $4,800 a year. If you were able to start this process at age nineteen as opposed to age twenty-six, the person who started at age nineteen could stop investing at age twenty-six and still make more money than the person who started later. All because of the magic of compound interest. Instead of walking you through all the numbers, let me show you what it looks like when you invest early! Here are a few examples to help show you how important it is to start early and lock your money into good investments.

Figure 1: Invested $400 a month from age nineteen to twenty-six, then stopped their monthly contributions

Figure 2: Invested $400 a month from age twenty-six to sixty-five

Figure 1: total gained is $3,103,188.33

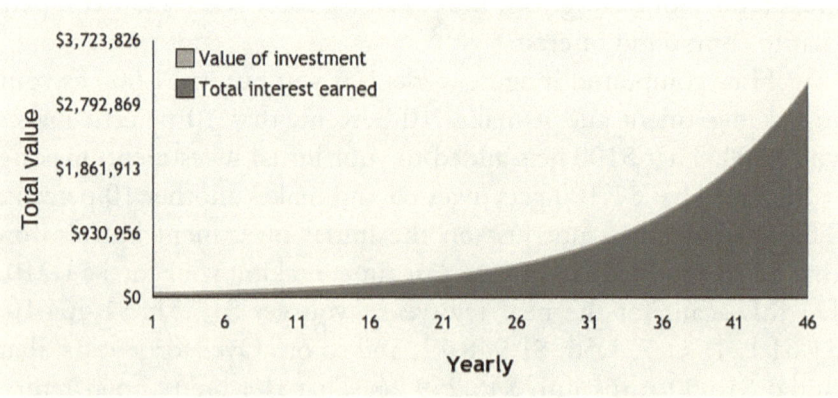

Figure 2: total gained is $2,028,139.00

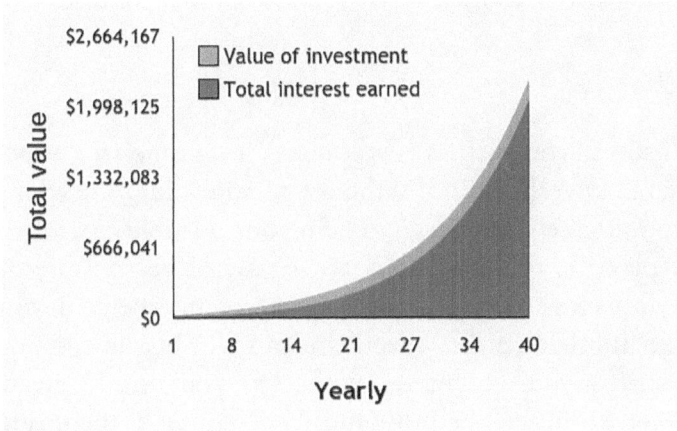

As you can see, the person in figure 1 started six years earlier but stopped their contributions at age twenty-six. Even though they stopped their contributions, they still managed to beat the other investor by $1,075,049.43. This is the power of investing early. The earlier you can start investing, the more time you give your money to grow and make your money make more money. Start now!

Know your investments

Knowing your investments does not mean you have to know every detail, but you need to know the basics and the risks associated with your investments. Never just take your buddy's advice, or even your financial advisor's advice; you need to know this for yourself. Your buddy may not know what they are talking about, and your financial advisor may be wanting their commission more than helping you. As a financial advisor myself, I know firsthand that there are broke and desperate people that work in this industry. My suggestion is to go to multiple advisors and look for someone who is willing to sit down with you and answer your questions. If you are constantly being pitched to, or you feel like you are being talked down to, move on to the next advisor. They need your business, but you do not need what they are selling; there are other advisors out there. Once you find an advisor you are comfortable with and you understand the investments as well as their risks, you are ready to start investing!

Diversify

Whatever you pick as investments, it is time to diversify that investment. Diversification is the art of spreading out your investments to mitigate your risks and help your portfolio perform better. Do not play the roulette wheel at Vegas and bet on one number. Spread your chips out, pick a grouping of numbers. If you catch the single number on the wheel, you can win big, but the odds are stacked against you. The more numbers you bet on, the greater your odds are of winning. The more numbers you pick, the greater your odds of coming out ahead in the end. Do not put all your eggs in one basket. If you choose mutual funds to invest in, make sure you buy a share in more than one mutual fund, in multiple sectors. If you invested in stocks, do not just buy one stock in one company; buy multiple stocks in multiple companies, in multiple countries, etc. The last layer of protection you want to add is your diversification of your risk levels. The higher your risk level, the higher reward potential, but this also means the greater potential of failure.

The higher risk you go, the more volatile the investment can be but also the larger your returns. At some point, the high risk investment or very aggressive investments can be up 20 percent or higher but then drop to 5 percent or lower. Having all your money in these types of investments can make your stress level rise and fall with them. You want some of your investments to be invested like this, but not all. You also want some aggressive risk, still wild but more stable than very aggressive funds. Put some in moderately aggressive and moderately conservative. The lower your risk, the lower your rate of potential return. This is why you need some in each risk level, so in the calm times, your aggressive funds can do what they do best, but when times are tough, your moderately conservative funds are stable and will stay more consistent through the storm. Spreading out your investments into these four risk levels will make your overall portfolio more stable.

Investments that don't pay

There is one more type of risk level, and that is conservative. Conservative investments are very low-risk and low-reward. When you invest in these types of investments, you are actually risking your investments not beating the average inflation rate. Inflation is the general increase of goods and services and the decrease of your money's value. The average inflation rate since 1915 has been just over 3 percent. On average, your $10 this year will not buy you as much as it could the year prior.

There are lots of investment choices to choose from, but some are just better than others. One of the main mistakes I see people make when they start investing is they find themselves in two different camps. Either they invest too aggressively in high-risk investments and end up losing, or they invest too conservatively or not aggressively enough and end up not surpassing the average inflation rate. You need to diversify your investments, and all your investments should be making you money.

Being too conservative

When you are investing, the last thing you want to do is not make money. The whole idea of investing is to make money and store it away for your future. Putting money in things like GICs (guaranteed investment certificate) or bonds, you are running the risk of not having your money make enough money back. If you do not make enough to cover inflation, you are technically losing money. We talked about inflation earlier, but inflation has historically gone up 3 percent every year. GICs, on average, make about a 2 percent rate of return and usually have to be locked in for at least a year to get that kind of return. I am no accountant, but 2 percent to 3 percent is equal to negative one. That is just a little bit better than keeping your money under the mattress. In fact, at least the money under your mattress is liquid and accessible; your money in a GIC is locked in, and you have the potential of losing all of its growth if you pull it out earlier than its maturity date.

Sure, a 2 percent rate of return is better than nothing, which is why it is so important that we distinguish between a saving rate of return and an investing rate of return. Investing in anything less than twice the inflation average is not worth the investment. Your investments can and will have a down year or two. This could get a lower rate of return than that, but over time, they will make a much better return. Even a moderately conservative fund like a safe mutual fund can make 6 percent growth on average. The nice thing about moderately conservative funds are they do not fluctuate nearly as much as your more aggressive funds. You are likely to see steady slow growth, with less negative effects because of the state of the market. In the wild times in the market, these funds feel a lot safer to be in. As the saying goes, "the higher the risk, the higher the reward." The opposite is also true. Low risk, low reward. You will never win in the investment world by playing things too safe.

Good, balanced returns

All your investments combined should produce an average return of 9 to 10 percent. The only way you can get there is to understand that extremely low-risk investments can produce a negative rate of return, and extremely high risk investments can produce a high rate of return. Both of these investments have the potential of making a zero-rate return. One carries risk by not being aggressive enough, and another carries risk by being too aggressive. Once you understand that going to either extreme is not a good financial move, it will help you understand why diversifying your portfolio is so important. When you diversify and put some moderately conservative investments in with some moderately aggressive, some aggressive, and some highly aggressive, you are more likely to make some consistent returns. You make sure your money actually makes you money. This will help to mitigate the risk of the high-risk investments and will help you get better rates of return.

Frequently invested

Being frequently in the market is key to winning regardless of if the market is up or down. The more frequently you can hit the market, the better average rate of return you can get. The term they use in the industry is dollar cost averaging. This is where you hit the market at different times throughout the year. You may be investing when the market is at its high point, but you may also hit the market at a low point. At the end of the year, you are more likely to get a better rate of return than trying to use the strategy of timing the market.

Timing the market is where you try to predict the market and invest when you think it is the right time. The most common strategy people use when timing the market is to invest when the market is low and sell when the market is high. When you try to time the market, you wind up missing opportunities. The more frequently you can hit the market, the better. In order for the dollar cost averaging strategy to work, you need to hit the market at least once a month, and better yet every two weeks. With how convenient online banking has become, you can have money automatically hit your account in whatever schedule you want it to. This allows you to simplify and automate this process, making investing easier. This will make sure you are always hitting the market at different times, as well as always being in the market. Think of this like a monthly membership that comes out of your account even though you do not use it, except that this membership is going toward your future.

Market consistency

Be consistent in the market. Don't let fear make your decisions. Leave your money in there. You wouldn't go into a clothing store, pick out a shirt, but when you get to the till, tell the cashier you will come back tomorrow when the sale is over to pay for it at full price. When the stock market takes a hit, human nature causes a small panic attack, which causes you to hold on to your money closer. Some go as far as pulling their money that was marked for their retirement and taking a huge loss. A better option would be to continue to hit the market frequently and stay in the market consistently. Stay consistent and resist the urge to pull from the market; let your money ride the waves. Being consistent in the market is all about staying in the market even when it takes a dip in the shallow end. The longer you can let it sit in the market, the more compound interest will grow your money for you!

The more frequently and consistently in the market, the better chances you are to take advantage of the market and make a better return overall. When you decide to make biweekly contributions instead of monthly contributions, this will increase your chances of being able to buy those investments while they are on sale. We are not timing the market; we are simply always in the market. Over time, this strategy will give you high rates of returns.

Investing above and beyond

You should never use timing the market as a strategy. The only time you should ever attempt to time the market is when you are already frequently and consistently in the market. When you have your dollar cost averaging strategy in place to hit the market randomly throughout the year, you may decide to throw some extra money in the market. Here are a couple guidelines to help you time the market wisely: Make sure whatever money you throw in, you are willing to lose. Do not take away from or limit your contributions from your consistency strategy. This money should be above that amount.

The problem with timing the market is people often use it as their only strategy and wind up taking big losses, missing opportunities, and/or pulling from their market early! Remember, investing is for the long-term. Your money needs time to compound and grow!

The only wrong time to be in the market is when you are not in it at all. The stock market has a long track record of making decent returns and over time has proven itself to climb its way back even with deep dips. Although the stock market is not the only place to invest in, it is a great starting point. As long as you remember these three rules of investing: know what you are investing in, diversify your investments, and be frequent and consistent in the market at all times.

Investment Vehicles

Before diving into these investment vehicles, I want to state that although this section is valuable, it is 100 percent Canadian material being covered. The vehicles themselves are easy enough to understand on their own, but if you are reading this as a non-Canadian, you may need to take some additional time to figure out similar products where you are at!

There are three main types of investment vehicles to choose from in Canada: registered retirement savings plan (RRSP), tax-free savings account (TFSA), and registered educational savings plan (RESP). There are lots of other vehicles out there, but these are the most common! The investment vehicle should not be mistaken for the investments themselves; they are simply the vehicle that protects the investments/drivers inside. Without the investments/drivers inside, these vehicles they are useless and provide no real benefit.

RRSP (REGISTERED RETIREMENT SAVINGS PLAN)

An RRSP is exactly what its name says it is. This vehicle's only purpose is for retirement. When you put your investments inside this vehicle, they get locked in until you are ready to retire. The first benefit to using this vehicle is it is a tax-deductible product. Whatever money you put into this vehicle, you can get a tax deduction from it, which will lower the amount of tax you owe at the end of the year. This product will also allow your investments to have tax-free growth inside the vehicle until you are ready to pull out the money from the account. When you are ready to withdraw your money, you are taxed on what you withdraw. As long as you do not pull this money out as a lump sum and instead pull it out in smaller increments that will keep your tax bill lower. At this point in your life, you are probably working less, and therefore, you will be in a lower tax bracket, keeping your tax bill lower again. This is a great option to take advantage of depending on your income situation. RRSPs let your money grow tax deferred till you are ready to retire. RRSPs are a very common vehicle used by employers to help them aid in their retirement and their staffs.

Ins and outs of RRSP.

For the most current information, I encourage you to visit your financial advisor to get the most up-to-date information. The concepts I am teaching you might not have an expiration date, but the specifics might have changed a bit. This is one of the most frequently asked questions I get: Can I have multiple RRSPs, and if so, is there a limit?

You are not limited to just one RRSP. You can have as many RRSPs as you want, but your contribution limit amount takes into account all of your RRSPs. For the year of 2020, the contribution limit was set at 18 percent of your earned income. There was also a capped dollar amount of $26,500 for the current year. This amount has been known to fluctuate from year to year, which is why they have a grace amount of $2,000 in place just in case you go over the amount above. If you do end up contributing to this vehicle, you will be subjected to a 1 percent penalty for every month that you over contributed. The only way to stop this fee from continuing is to withdraw the extra money and be subjected to the tax consequences. Whenever you have to withdraw from your RRSP, you will be taxed. If you do not use all your contribution room from the years previous, you can add that room to your current year's contributions with no penalty.

Spouse-contributed RRSP.

If you have a spouse or common law partner, you can open up a spousal RRSP and both contribute to each other's RRSPs to maximize this investment vehicle. This works out well if you have one high-income earner and the other one low. The higher income earner can decide to fill up their contribution level first and then add to their spouse's after theirs is maxed out. This will help maximize your contribution limits and will allow you to get a larger tax deduction.

TFSA (TAX-FREE SAVING ACCOUNT)

THE TFSA IS A great investment vehicle as it is less restrictive compared to the RRSP and is not specifically set up for retirement. The TFSA is a post-tax product, which means that the tax has already been taken out before it goes into the vehicle. After your money is put into your investments inside this vehicle, the money grows tax-free. The nice thing about this vehicle is when you are ready to pull your money out, you can pull it out with no tax implications. This vehicle is also less restrictive, so you can pull your money out early to use if needed, for things like your house down payment or to start a business. The problem with having less restrictions in this vehicle is it can be tempting to pull out your money early and spend it rather than keep it invested. Another thing to just be aware of is that your investments inside this account may have restrictions or penalties for pulling out the money, but these are usually front-end loaded, and by a certain period of time, they will disappear. It is so important to know why you are investing your money so you are less tempted to use it for "fun." This vehicle is a great vehicle to use for retirement but can also be used for other investment purposes.

Ins and outs of TFSA.

The TFSA is a newer vehicle as it was first created in 2009. You have to be eighteen years of age to start contributing to your TFSA, and it carries a yearly contribution amount. The TFSA, like the RRSP, has no limit to how many TFSAs you have, just the dollar amount of all the accounts combined. Contribution limits to a TFSA vary from year to year but have been around $6,000 a year, with the ability to max out your contributions from your previous years. As an example, if you turned eighteen any time after 2009, your total contribution would be $75,500. Unlike the RRSP, TFSA cannot be contributed to by a spouse; they are always kept as separate entities. For the most current numbers and information, please visit your financial advisor or your tax professional. These are just examples to illustrate how it works.

Which one is better?

Before we move on to RESPs, I want to take a moment to compare these two vehicles. Both of these vehicles are great for retirement and allow your money to grow tax-free. People often ask me which one to invest in first. My answer is always both. Do not limit your investing potential by trying to invest as little as possible. I want you to kick-start both investment vehicles, but then after you start them both, I want you to focus on maxing one out before adding to the other.

Like the other three negotiables, you are constantly building up disciplines to keep yourself winning and not falling off the wagon and giving up. The RRSP is a great place to start as all your contributions into it get locked, and with all the taxes and fees it would cost to pull it out early, you are less tempted to use that money for other purposes. When you are just starting out on your investing journey, using this vehicle is wise, as if storms do come with everything you have been taught above, and the restrictions of the vehicle itself will stop you from doing something financially unwise. This does not mean I only want you to use this vehicle, but it's a good place to start, especially for your first year of investing.

The strategy I recommend more often than not is this: Start to contribute 10 percent to your RRSP to limit your risk of pulling out early and to get your tax deduction. When you get your tax return back, put the majority of your tax return into a TFSA and get that vehicle started. By contributing to your RRSP, you have already committed that money to go toward retirement, so your tax return should be doing double time and making you more money. By putting it back into a retirement account, you can take full advantage of the money you put into your RRSP. Depending on your income level or marital status, your advisor may advise you to keep contributing to your RRSP or switch contributions to your TFSA. I do want you to run both vehicles side by side, but I want you to max them out one at a time. This will allow you to have a bigger pile of money compounding for your future rather than two smaller piles. At this point, you are either choosing to put your contributions in one or the other until it is maxed out, then you can start contributions to the other one. Again, depending on your situation, this could be either one.

Instead of getting caught up in the details of which one would be better for you to max out first, the bigger picture is that you are investing! Understand the vehicles and their pros and cons, max one out before the other, but then commit and start investing. Do not limit your future-investing potential because one advisor told you to invest in your TFSA and another advisor told you to invest in your RRSP. Both are good vehicles and should be utilized. Now let's move on to RESPs.

RESP (REGISTERED EDUCATION SAVINGS PLAN)

The RESP, like the RRSP, has a specific purpose or use for this vehicle. This one's for education. There are three types of plans inside the RESP. The first plan is a family plan. This plan is ideal if you have more than one child. The children must be related to you or adopted to be added to this plan. If one child does not go to post-secondary education, it can be transferred to the other siblings. The next plan is the individual plan (nonfamily) plan. This plan is ideal for saving for unrelated children. You are wanting to save for their education. The last opinion is a group plan RESP. This plan is ideal for one person and does not have to be related to get it. With any of these plans, depending on how much you invest into the plan and your income level, you could get a government grant. These plans can be contributed to for thirty-one years and need to be withdrawn or used by year thirty-five. The contributions grow tax-free, and only the interest your money earns is taxed when withdrawn.

Limitations of RESP.

Like the TFSA and RRSP, the contributions into this vehicle will grow tax-free. The biggest difference between this vehicle and the other two is there is a possible contribution limit in the form of a grant from the government. Depending on your income level and the amount you contribute each year, the grant could be as much as $7,200 to sit and grow tax-free. The government will match up to 20 percent of your first $2,500 and up to $500 per beneficiary each year after. Your maximum contribution limit for thirty-one years is $50,000 per beneficiary. Whatever interest income your account makes will be considered taxable income for the student/beneficiary of the money withdrawn for school. This is a non-tax-deductible product, and the interest growth is taxed when withdrawn.

If for whatever reason, the beneficiary decides not to go to school, depending on the plan, that money could be transferred to another beneficiary. If this is not an option, you will have to roll it over to your RRSP or cash it out. In either one of these options, your grants received from the government will be returned. If you decide to cash out the policy, you will be taxed on the income interest it made while inside the account and will be subjected to a 20 percent penalty on that amount as well. This vehicle is a great option if you want to have the government contribute financially to your child's education, but again, please consult with your advisor to make sure you choose the proper plan for you!

For you to really know if these concepts are working in your life, it does take some time, so be patient. It takes about three months to get your monthly budget all figured out, but then after that, it is small tweaks from month to month to keep you going. It takes you about three to six months to see the results of giving first and how that discipline can and does change your life; be patient. When it comes to paying down your debt, you will find that the first few debts are the hardest to conquer and the easiest to give up on. Keep pushing. The journey may not get any easier, but you will feel like you are winning, which will motivate you to finish!

Key points of *Investing*:

After you are out of consumer debt, start investing 10 percent.

Know and understand what your investments
- Don't just trust one advisor or your know-it-all uncle; ask around and learn the basics.

Diversify your investments
- Spread them out from different areas in the market to different risk levels; don't put all your eggs in one basket.
- There is such a thing as being too aggressive and too conservative; get a good balance and make sure your investments payoff.

Be frequent in the market
- The more times you can hit the market, the more chances you have of making a better return.
- Don't try to time the market; just simply always be in the market.

Be consistent in the Market
- Don't pull out of the market early! Let your investments ride the waves.
- Compound interest is an amazing thing, but it needs time to work.

Check with a local professional to see your options and how you can get started investing!

Tips and Tricks

In this last section, I wanted to compile the top tips and tricks I have collected from real people about finance. Some of the names have been changed for privacy purposes, but this is real raw advice from people who believe in these disciplines and have implemented them into their everyday life.

Give:

- Give openly without expectations. You limit your opportunities when you constrict your expectations. (Manprete)
- Structure your giving, but also put some money aside to be spontaneous in your giving. You never know who you can impact when you plan to give. (Rylie)
- If you don't put giving first on your budget, you are limiting your potential to be a part of something bigger than yourself! (Simone)
- Don't settle by just giving your minimum. Stretch yourself and see the change it will make. (Sarah)
- Transfer the amount you plan to give to a separate account. That way, you are less likely to spend it instead of giving it away. (Alex)
- Give in secret. This will help you stay humble and help you understand what giving is actually all about. (Eurgon)
- If you give and get a tax refund from your giving, I encourage part of that money for yourself but then to give from that amount as well. (Greg)

- If you have kids, show them what it looks like to be generous and give. If you "tip the bill," make sure you leave the table before the waitress gets there, and tell your kids to watch for her reaction. You just changed more than one person's life that day. (Samatha)
- Be on the same page with your spouse about where you are giving and how much you want to give. This will stretch one of you to become more generous and align your lives that much more. (Trisha)
- Giving is less about the amount that you give and more about the impact you made. (Rosa)

Live:

- If you struggle with guilt by not being able to pay your credit card bill because you have to put food on the table first, don't. The credit card industry makes billions of dollars a year. They don't care about your family. (Owen)
- Your mental health is more important than your financial well-being. You can't help yourself or your family if you aren't mentally healthy. (Rachel)
- One of the benefits to buying everything used is that you can often resell it at a very similar price to what you paid for it when you upgrade. Don't be ashamed of buying used. It's a great way to save money. (Aly)
- Drive your beater car with pride, and give it a name. If someone hits it or scratches it, it will bother you less, and because it's not worth fixing the minor stuff, you will save money. (Spence)
- Remember to take time just to be with your family. It might delay your financial journey a bit, but it will also help you remember that your family is more important than money. (Loyd)
- List out all your subscriptions (you probably have more than you think), then choose one or two and cut the rest. (Barb)

- DIY is a great option to save money. Just make sure your project actually saves you money. Count the cost first! (Geni)
- If you are a big coffee drinker, consider buying a higher-end coffee machine. They may cost more in the beginning, but if you stop going out for coffee because of it, you will save money in the long run. (Mike)

Paying off debt:

- Give yourself grace. It's so easy to fall into debt, but it takes a lot of hard work to get out. (Byron)
- Don't invest while getting out of debt. Every extra dollar you have needs to go to paying off your debt. Be patient; you can invest later! (William)
- Personal nonnegotiables are key. They keep you motivated. Just be careful not to overspend!
- Don't take the easy way out like debt consolidation: it's a temporary fix, and it will not help you build the discipline you need to win. (Shawn)
- Be motivated by other people's stories, but don't compare. Everyone's journey is different. (Eddy)

Life insurance:

- Only buy term insurance; it's very affordable and you can actually get the coverage you need for a fraction of the cost. (Jason)
- Get life insurance as soon as possible. You never know what the future holds, and the sooner you get it, the cheaper your rates will be. (Zahid)
- Do not just go to one life insurance agent. Shop around and pick one that you feel comfortable with. (Gavin)
- Even if you can't afford the amount you need, get something in place today. A little bit of life insurance is better than no life insurance. (Randal)

- There are a lot of upsells in insurance. Make sure you are covered, but make sure you are not being nickel and dimed to death; do your research. (Devin)

Save:

- Separate your savings from your checking account. There is less temptation to spend. (Vay)
- Always have a float in your account of a few hundred dollars so that you don't go into overdraft. (Tim)
- Use sinking funds as much as possible. Even having an anonymous sinking fund is a good idea to not get caught not having enough saved. (Greg)
- Using a "do not pay for 180 days" is not a savings plan. Whatever you do, make sure you have the money in the bank, and pay for it right away. (Daltyn)
- Like anything in life, if you don't make it a priority, you won't do it. Start by saving even $5 a week! (Shaggy)
- Get creative; put your emergency fund in a piggy bank and seal it so you have to break it to get at your money. This will help you determine what an emergency actually is! (Sandra)
- Pack a lunch! You will save thousands of dollars a year! (William)
- Plan your vacations early. When you make a sinking fund, give yourself two months extra to make sure you have covered all the costs of the trip! (Cohlhan)
- Don't buy a brand-new car! Buy a two-year-old or older car. It has already lost 40 percent of its value, essentially giving you a 40 percent discount! Oh, and pay cash. No payments! (Ann)
- If you bank online, have the app notify you every time you spend. You will save money just by wanting it to stop! (Victor)

Other Disciplines:

- Do not borrow money from your relatives. It complicates relationships and has potential to cause bitterness. (Shelby)
- Learn to say no even when you want to say yes. Be future-focused instead of now-focused. (Henry)
- Create humility. The more humility you have, the easier it is to be content with what you have and not compare with others. (Luci)
- Budget. When you learn how to budget, you learn how to control your money! (Kayley)
- Purchase wisely. Ask yourself what you really need instead of saying, "How much can I stretch my budget for?" (Bella)

About the Author

Randy Bowen is a common-sense, no-nonsense financial learner, teacher, and legacy coach. He's a learner because teaching finances was never on his radar or in his future plans. It took him falling into the debt trap and learning how to navigate his own finances to wake up and see the real need we have as a society to get our finances right. As he learns more and more, he realizes how overwhelming understanding finances can feel and how backward finances are taught in today's society. He's also a financial teacher because after he researched and navigated the financial world, he was able to understand the complexities and has the ability to simplify them for everyone to grasp and understand. Finally, he is a legacy coach because nothing brings him more joy than seeing someone starting to win in their finances and start to build a legacy for them and their family. Through research, hard work, and good old trial and error, Randy has found some common financial struggles and created some simple, counterintuitive disciplines and solutions to help everyone start to win in their finances.

www.ingramcontent.com/pod-product-compliance
Lightning Source LLC
Chambersburg PA
CBHW030814180526
45163CB00003B/1275